Great Taste ~ Low Fat

DESSERTS

TIME
LIFE
BOOKS

ALEXANDRIA, VIRGINIA

TABLE OF CONTENTS

Brownies

page 33

Raspberry Pie

page 55

Frozen Desserts

Crumbles, Crêpes, Etc.

INTRODUCTION

Our mission at Great Taste-Low Fat is to take the work and worry out of everyday low-fat cooking; to provide delicious, fresh, and filling recipes for family and friends; to use quick, streamlined methods and available ingredients; and, within every recipe, to keep the percentage of calories from fat under 30 percent.

Do you subscribe to the sentiment, "Life is short—eat dessert first"? Do you cherish a collection of favorite family recipes for cookies and cakes? Are you the "designated baker" for birthday parties? Then you've probably put some thought into the problem of how to make tempting desserts that are lower in fat.

PRACTICE MAKES PERFECT

Low-fat desserts would be a snap if you could simply eliminate the fat from your favorite recipes, but you can't just remove the butter from pie crust, the cream from mousse, or the chocolate from brownies, without making some careful calculations, modifications, and substitutions. Fat performs many important functions in desserts: It tenderizes baked goods, helps them rise, and keeps them moist and fresh. And, fat gives all sorts of desserts a luxurious richness—it makes delectable flavors like chocolate, butterscotch, or lemon linger pleasurably in your mouth. When our chef, Sandy Gluck, sat down to create the recipes in this book, she knew that most people have a very clear and specific image of the flavors and textures of their favorite desserts: This expectation meant that classic desserts couldn't be changed too drastically, or they would surely disappoint. And Sandy was well aware that dessert-making—especially

baking—is a fairly exact science, unlike soup-making, for example. You can't just take out the shortening and eggs and hope for the best. Even more than usual, the recipes in this book required testing and retesting, tasting and sampling. "It takes a number of trials to figure out whether you can leave out three egg yolks or just two, how much fat you can cut from a pie crust or cookie dough, whether evaporated skimmed milk needs a bit of sour cream to enrich it when it stands in for heavy cream. There was a lot of fine-tuning involved." Knowing how fat intensifies the perception of flavors, Sandy also worked to "pump up" flavors that pale when fat is cut. For instance, lemon zest reinforces the flavor of lemon juice, and instant espresso replaces regular instant coffee.

MEETING THE CHALLENGE

You may be pleasantly surprised when you take a look at the recipes we've come up with. There's a coconut cream pie (made with fewer egg yolks and less coconut than usual, its flavor reinforced with coconut extract); two cheesecakes (reduced-fat cream cheese and cottage cheese stand in for regular cream cheese); and a chocolate-glazed three-layer fudge cake with just 8 grams of fat per serving. In this "to-die-for" dessert, nonfat sour cream compensates for a reduced amount of butter; cocoa powder takes the place of most of the solid chocolate; and egg whites replace some of the whole eggs. For a simpler, but equally satisfying, treat try our brownies, in which prune purée replaces much of the shortening; the purée's rich flavor also heightens the chocolate flavor.

Certain desserts didn't need much tinkering with because they were already low in fat or fat-free. Poached fruit, compote, sorbet, granita, frozen yogurt, cornstarch-thickened pudding, and angel food cake are among these healthy classics. We concentrated on keeping them healthy and making them as tasty as they could possibly be.

Although some recipes in this book take more time than other Great Taste~Low Fat recipes, it's frequently "hands-off" time that you can devote to other things while a dessert is baking, cooling, or chilling. Our "Secrets of Low-Fat Desserts" section explains low-fat substitutions, describes (and shows) some dessert-making techniques, illustrates plain and fancy baking equipment, and offers a battery of basic recipes.

Need some extra incentive to get started? Just imagine the delighted reactions when you bring out one of these homemade desserts. If someone says, "No thanks—too rich!" you can proudly reply, "Help yourself, it's low in fat!"

CONTRIBUTING EDITORS

Sandra Rose Gluck, a New York City chef, has years of experience creating delicious low-fat recipes that are quick to prepare. Her secret for satisfying results is to always aim for great taste and variety. By combining readily available, fresh ingredients with simple cooking techniques, Sandra has created the perfect recipes for today's busy lifestyles.

Grace Young has been the director of a major test kitchen specializing in low-fat and health-related cookbooks for over 12 years. Grace oversees the development, taste testing, and nutritional analysis of every recipe in Great Taste~Low Fat. Her goal is simple: take the work and worry out of low-fat cooking so that you can enjoy delicious, healthy meals every day.

Kate Slate has been a food editor for almost 20 years, and has published thousands of recipes in cookbooks and magazines. As the Editorial Director of Great Taste~Low Fat, Kate combined simple, easy to follow directions with practical low-fat cooking tips. The result is guaranteed to make your low-fat cooking as rewarding and fun as it is foolproof.

NUTRITION

Every recipe in *Great Taste~Low Fat* provides per-serving values for the nutrients listed in the chart at right. The daily intakes listed in the chart are based on those recommended by the USDA and presume a nonsedentary lifestyle. The nutritional emphasis in this book is not only on controlling calories, but on reducing total fat grams. Research has shown that dietary fat metabolizes more easily into body fat than do carbohydrates and protein. In order to control the amount of fat in a given recipe and in your diet in general, no more than 30 percent of the calories should come from fat.

Nutrient	Women	Men
Fat	<65 g	<80 g
Calories	2000	2500
Saturated fat	<20 g	<25 g
Carbohydrate	300 g	375 g
Protein	50 g	65 g
Cholesterol	<300 mg	<300 mg
Sodium	<2400 mg	<2400 mg

These recommended daily intakes are averages used by the Food and Drug Administration and are consistent with the labeling on all food products. Although the values for cholesterol and sodium are the same for all adults, the other intake values vary depending on gender, ideal weight, and activity level. Check with a physician or nutritionist for your own daily intake values.

SECRETS OF LOW-FAT DESSERTS

DESSERTS

Low-fat dessert-making comes with its own unique challenges, but a little know-how combined with the right recipe will give you great results. That's why we've complemented our recipes with an expanded "Secrets" section. Here you'll find the best ingredient substitutions; detailed preparation techniques; photographic features on both essential and specialized equipment; and seven "basic" recipes for sensational low-fat fillings, crusts, and toppings used in recipes throughout the book—you can use them to lighten your own favorite desserts, too.

LOW-FAT INGREDIENTS

Our main objective with dessert recipes is to cut fat, while still preserving flavor and texture. One way we did this was through the use of low-fat substitutions. Applesauce and prune purée are two amazing fat replacements for baking: Soluble fiber and other substances in these fruits supply baked goods with the moistness and tenderness that usually come from fat. Corn syrup can also replace some fat in simple cakes and cookies (it makes for smoother frozen desserts, too), as can reduced-fat cream cheese and nonfat or low-fat yogurt. While it's hard to bake without eggs, egg whites (which have no fat or cholesterol) can be substituted for

whole eggs: Often, we use one whole egg plus one or more whites to replace additional whole eggs (yolks make baked goods tender, and without them, some cakes and cookies would be dry and hard). We often substitute cocoa powder—chocolate minus the fat—for solid chocolate. Chocolate chips are a convenient form of solid chocolate: They needn't be chopped for either melting or for mixing into batters. When chips are used whole, we use mini chips, which give the impression of more chocolate per bite.

Flavorings are especially important in low-fat cooking. We use a wide variety—from spices, extracts, and liqueurs to espresso powder, vanilla beans, and citrus zest. Be sure that your spices are fresh and use pure, not imitation, extracts.

Low-fat and fat-free dairy products let you serve more healthful puddings, pie fillings, and frostings. Low-fat buttermilk gives cakes a tender crumb, while reduced-fat sour cream can often stand in for whipped cream. Low-fat cream cheese can replace some of the butter in pastries and cakes, and drained nonfat yogurt imitates soft cream cheese. You can use low-fat or skimmed evaporated milk instead of heavy cream and cut hundreds of grams of fat while creating wonderfully creamy desserts.

DESSERT TECHNIQUES

Accuracy is more important in baking than in other types of cooking. Oven temperature, for instance, is critical. An oven thermometer (sold at housewares stores) will show whether your oven controls are accurate. If not, you can have the controls recalibrated: Even a fairly new oven can be inaccurate. For proper rising, don't open the oven during the first 15 minutes of baking a cake; after that, open and close the door quickly but gently. Use a timer to spare yourself the frustration and waste of burned baked goods. Follow the directions for cooling and removing cakes and cookies from the pan—removed too soon, they can crumble, and left in the pan too long, they may stick.

Some cake and cookie recipes require you to sift flour, which aerates and lightens it. You don't need a flour sifter to do this: Place the flour in a sieve and shake it, gently pushing the flour through with a wooden spoon as necessary. When the directions call for flouring a pan, don't take the flour from the measured amount called for in the recipe; use a few pinches of additional flour.

Measure carefully: Especially in baking, the proportions of ingredients—of baking powder to flour or liquid ingredients to dry—must be care-

continued on page 8

1 Rolling pin. A large, heavy rolling pin with ball bearings works most smoothly.

2 Square metal baking pan. The standard size for bar cookies is 8 inches.

3, 4 Deep-dish pie plate and pie weights. Place the weights on a piece of foil on top of the dough when baking an unfilled crust.

5 Ceramic pie plate. This is interchangeable with heatproof glass pie plates.

6 Wire cooling rack. This rack is perfect for cakes; use a larger rack for cookies.

7 Glass custard cups. The 6-ounce size is perfect for single-serving desserts.

8 Ceramic ramekins. These are for individual dessert soufflés or puddings.

9 Parchment paper. This works well for lining cookie sheets and cake pans.

10 Cake pan. We use 8-inch round cake pans with straight sides and a dull finish.

11 Pastry blender. Use this tool to blend shortening or butter into dry ingredients.

12 Rubber spatula. Better than a spoon for folding in delicate ingredients.

13 Pastry brush. For glazing and for removing crumbs from a cake before frosting.

14 Glass baking dish. A shallow baking dish is just right for cobblers and the like.

15, 16 Coarse- and fine-mesh sieves. Use a coarse sieve for sifting flour or confectioners' sugar, the fine sieve for straining purées.

17 Jelly-roll pan. A baking sheet with sides good for bar cookies and sheet cakes.

18 Muffin pan. With a nonstick pan, you don't need to use paper liners.

19 Cookie sheet. The rimless sheet is best for cookies; no sides means easier removal.

fully balanced for good results. And because un-cooked batter or dough is so different from the finished product, it's hard to gauge what effect any improvisation or guesswork might have. You'll need two kinds of measuring cups for these recipes. Use a set of graduated cups for dry ingredients—usually including ¼-cup, ⅓-cup, ½-cup and 1 cup. For liquids, use a clear glass or plastic cup with markings on the side. To measure dry ingredients, fill the cup to overflowing then level the contents (see "Measuring Dry Ingredients" be-low). To measure liquids, place the cup on the counter and fill to the appropriate mark, then bend over to view the measurement at eye level.

It's a good practice to stir flour a bit before mea-suring it. When you open a fresh bag of flour, dump it into a large canister or other container to separate the flour particles, which will have be-come compacted in the bag.

Always use eggs graded "large" when preparing the recipes in this book. To separate an egg, crack it, then drop the yolk from half-shell to half-shell, letting the white fall into a bowl—or use an inex-pensive egg separator. Eggs separate more easily when cold, but beat up to fuller volume at room temperature; if time allows, separate the eggs straight out of the refrigerator, then let the whites stand for a few minutes before beating. Cream of tartar, sometimes added to egg whites before beat-ing, makes the beaten whites firmer and more sta-ble. When folding beaten whites into batter, first "lighten" the batter by folding in a few spoonfuls

Measuring Dry Ingredients

To measure a light, fine ingredient such as flour, use a scoop to overfill the measuring cup. Then, with a table knife, level the contents. Don't dip the measuring cup into the flour and don't shake or tap the cup to level the contents (this will compact the flour). You can, however, use the dipping method to measure granulated sugar.

Beating Egg Whites

Be sure that the bowl and beaters are clean and grease-free: Just a speck of yolk will keep egg whites from beating up well. With the mixer at slow speed, beat the whites (and cream of tartar, if the recipe calls for it) un-til they resemble a thick, foamy syrup.

Increase the mixer speed to medium and beat until the egg whites are thick and fine-textured. You should be able to mound the whites in rounded peaks, but they will still look quite wet. If you tilt the bowl, the beat-en whites will slide around.

Increase the mixer speed to high and contin-ue beating (gradually adding sugar, if the recipe calls for it) until the egg whites hold stiff peaks when the beaters are lifted. Be sure not to overbeat; the whites should look satin-smooth and glossy, not dry.

of egg white. And when adding eggs to a hot mixture (such as milk that has been scalded for custard), first "temper" the eggs by stirring in a little hot milk; otherwise, the eggs might curdle.

A few of our recipes are made with meringue—sweetened, stiffly beaten egg whites. Meringues are sensitive to humidity, so they're best made on a clear, dry day. It's a good idea to use superfine sugar (an extra-fine granulated sugar, not to be confused with confectioners') for meringues be-cause it blends easily with the egg whites. You can, however, substitute regular granulated.

Some of our recipes have you grease a pan with nonstick cooking spray, while for others you're di-rected to grease and flour or line the pan with waxed paper. There are reasons for these distinc-tions: For low-fat cookies, the baking sheet must be greased to keep the cookies from sticking; oversized, thin, or fragile cookies are often baked on waxed paper or parchment so that the cookies don't break as you remove them. Greased and floured waxed paper protects delicate cakes, which, if they stuck to the pan, might fall apart.

When flouring a pan, rotate and shake it to cover the greased surface evenly with flour, then tap the pan and shake out any excess. Pans for angel food cakes should not be greased or floured: The batter (made with only beaten egg whites for leavening) needs a "nonslip" surface to climb or the cake won't rise properly. It's easiest to get cupcakes out of the pan if you use paper liners, but you can use nonstick spray instead, if you prefer.

Melting Chocolate

The time needed to microwave chocolate varies with the amount. For 2 ounces chips, cook on high power for 1 minute, then check by stir-ring (the chips will appear unchanged). If not melted, continue in 10-second intervals. For smaller amounts, start with 30 seconds.

To melt chocolate chips on the stovetop, bring a small pot of water to a simmer. Place the chips in a heatproof bowl and set the bowl over the saucepan (the water should not touch the bottom of the bowl). Turn the heat off and stir until the chips are melted and smooth.

Lining a Cake Pan

Place the cake pan on a sheet of waxed paper or parchment and trace around the bottom of the pan (not the top, which is generally wider) with a pencil. If using waxed paper, you can scratch the outline of the pan onto the paper with the tip of a knife.

Cut out the shape, cutting slightly inside the line. If you are are using two or more pans, stack multiple layers of paper and cut them all at once (a staple in the center of the stack will prevent sliding as you cut). Spray the pan with nonstick spray and fit the paper into the pan.

BASIC RECIPES

These pie crusts, custards, frostings, and toppings are called for in some of the recipes in this book. You can also use them as starting points for your own creative low-fat desserts. When one of these "basics" appears as part of a dessert recipe, the total time given for the whole recipe will include the time required for preparing the basic recipe, as well.

Basic Pie Dough

In this recipe, cream cheese and nonfat yogurt take the place of some of the fat normally used in pie dough. The result is a crust that's light and flaky yet rich-tasting. Be careful not to overmix the dough; cut in the shortening with quick strokes, and stir the mixture as little as possible after adding the yogurt. Chilling the dough before rolling it out makes it easier to handle.

1 cup flour
2 tablespoons granulated sugar
¼ teaspoon salt
¼ teaspoon baking powder
¼ cup solid vegetable shortening
2 tablespoons cream cheese
⅓ cup plain nonfat yogurt

1. In a medium bowl, combine the flour, sugar, salt, and baking powder, stirring until well combined. With a pastry blender or two knives, cut in the shortening and cream cheese until the mixture resembles coarse meal. Stir the yogurt into the flour mixture until just moistened. Shape the dough into a flat disk, wrap in plastic wrap, and refrigerate for at least 1 hour.

2. On a lightly floured surface, roll the dough out to a 13-inch circle. Center the dough in a 9-inch deep-dish glass or ceramic pie plate. Fold any overhang in, then form a high fluted edge (see photo). Prick the dough several times with a fork.

3. Preheat the oven to 375°. Line the pie shell with foil and pour pie weights or dried beans into the foil. Bake for 10 minutes, or until just set. Remove the weights and foil and bake for 10 minutes, or until golden brown. Cool on a wire rack.

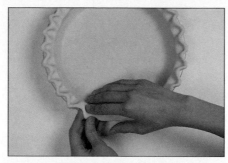

Pinch the edge of the dough between your fingers to make a fluted edge.

Line the pie shell with a sheet of foil, then cover the bottom with pie weights or dried beans.

For a tart, fold the overhang in to make a sturdy wall of dough, gently pressing it into the flutes.

Basic Cookie Crust

It's easy to lighten the standard graham-cracker crust: We use about half as much fat and moisten the mixture with milk.

9 ounces cookies (see variations below)
2 tablespoons granulated sugar
4 teaspoons vegetable oil
¼ cup low-fat (1%) milk

1. Preheat the oven to 375°. In a food processor, process the cookies and sugar until finely ground. Add the oil and milk and process until thoroughly moistened.

2. Spray a 9-inch glass or ceramic pie plate with nonstick cooking spray. Press the crumb mixture into the bottom and up the sides of the prepared pie plate. Bake for 10 minutes. Cool on a wire rack.

VARIATIONS

Graham Cracker: Use 36 individual graham cracker squares (2⅜ x 2⅜).
Chocolate-Graham: Use 36 individual graham cracker squares (2⅜ x 2⅜) and add 2 tablespoons of unsweetened cocoa powder.
Toasted Oatmeal-Graham: Use 24 individual graham cracker squares (2⅜ x 2⅜) and ½ cup of old-fashioned rolled oats. Toast the oats in a 375° oven for 7 minutes, or until lightly crisped.
Gingersnap: Use 36 gingersnaps.
Crunchy Gingersnap: Use 28 gingersnaps and ½ cup of crunchy nugget cereal (such as grape-nuts).
Butterscotch: Use 48 reduced-fat vanilla wafers and brown sugar in place of the granulated sugar.

Vanilla Pastry Cream

Pastry cream, or *crème pâtissière,* is a thick custard that's used as a filling for layer cakes and for pastries such as éclairs and cream puffs. Pastry cream is traditionally a flour-thickened mixture, so the whole egg and butter here serve mostly to provide a touch of richness and, of course, buttery flavor. (The standard recipe calls for 4 egg yolks and 2 tablespoons of butter.) Prepare the pastry cream about an hour in advance (or up to one day ahead of time) to allow it time to cool completely. The plastic wrap placed on the surface of the cream prevents a skin from forming as it cools.

⅓ cup granulated sugar
1 tablespoon plus 2 teaspoons flour
1 cup low-fat (1%) milk
1 large egg
2 teaspoons unsalted butter
1 teaspoon vanilla extract

1. In a small, heavy-bottomed saucepan, whisk together the sugar and flour. Gradually whisk in the milk and bring to a boil over medium heat. Remove from the heat. In a small bowl, lightly beat the egg. Gradually whisk some of the hot milk mixture into the egg, then whisk the warmed egg mixture back into the saucepan.

2. Bring the mixture to a boil over medium heat and cook for 1 minute, whisking constantly. Reduce the heat to a simmer and cook, whisking constantly, until the filling is thick enough to heavily coat a spoon. Remove from the heat and stir in the butter and vanilla. Pour the filling into a bowl, place plastic wrap directly on the surface, and refrigerate until ready to use.

Vanilla Custard Sauce

This versatile sauce, sometimes called English custard or *crème anglaise,* makes something special of simple cakes such as gingerbread. It's also great over fresh berries, warm compote, baked apples or pears, and other fruit desserts.

1 cup low-fat (1%) milk
⅓ cup granulated sugar
1 large egg
1 teaspoon vanilla extract

1. In a small saucepan, combine the milk and sugar and bring to a simmer over medium heat. Remove from the heat. In a small bowl, lightly beat the egg. Gradually whisk some of the hot milk mixture into the egg, then whisk the warmed egg mixture back into the saucepan.

2. Cook the sauce over low heat, whisking constantly (do not boil), until it's thick enough to lightly coat a spoon, 10 to 15 minutes. Cool to room temperature and stir in the vanilla. Transfer the sauce to a bowl, place plastic wrap directly on the surface, and refrigerate until ready to use.

When the custard sauce is done, it should be thick enough to lightly coat a metal spoon.

Sugar Glazes and Drizzles

This basic vanilla glaze recipe and its orange and lemon variations are thick enough to spread with a spatula. The "drizzles," however, are thin and pourable: When spooned over a cake, they'll drip down the sides. The difference is in the amount of liquid used. When preparing either a glaze or a drizzle, if the mixture is too thick for your purpose, simply add more of the appropriate liquid. Add just ½ teaspoon at a time: It takes a very small amount to make a difference.

1 cup confectioners' sugar
1 teaspoon vanilla extract
4 teaspoons low-fat (1%) milk

In a small bowl, combine the sugar, vanilla, and milk.

VARIATIONS

Orange Glaze: Omit the vanilla and milk and use 4 teaspoons of orange juice.
Orange Drizzle: Omit the vanilla and milk and use 2 tablespoons of orange juice.
Lemon Glaze: Omit the vanilla and milk and use 4 teaspoons of lemon juice and 1 teaspoon grated lemon zest.
Lemon Drizzle: Omit the vanilla and milk and use 2 tablespoons of lemon juice and 1 teaspoon grated lemon zest.
Lemon-Ginger Drizzle: Omit the vanilla and milk and use 4 teaspoons of lemon juice, 1 teaspoon grated lemon zest, and 2 teaspoons ginger juice. (To make ginger juice, grate a 3-inch piece of unpeeled ginger into a bowl and, with your hands, squeeze the grated ginger to extract as much juice as possible.)

Vanilla Yogurt Topping

The simple process of draining the whey from yogurt transforms it into a thick, tangy substitute for whipped cream, *crème fraîche,* sour cream, or cream cheese, depending on the length of time it's allowed to drain. After 3 hours of draining, the yogurt will be roughly as thick as sour cream; you'll have a little more than ½ cup. This creamy yogurt can be used, plain or with additional flavoring, as a spoonable topping. After 6 hours of draining, you'll have a yogurt "cheese" about as thick as cream cheese; the yield will be a little less than ½ cup.

8 ounces vanilla low-fat yogurt

1. Set a paper-lined coffee filter, or a sieve lined with 2 layers of paper towels or dampened cheesecloth, over a bowl. Spoon the yogurt into the prepared utensil.

2. Cover the yogurt with a small plate or a sheet of plastic wrap and refrigerate for 3 to 6 hours, depending on the desired thickness. Discard the whey.

Three options for draining yogurt: A coffee filter with a paper liner; a sieve lined with paper towels; a sieve lined with cheesecloth.

Cream Cheese Frosting

Thick, sweet, cream cheese frosting doesn't have to be a thing of the past just because you're cutting down on fat. A combination of nonfat and reduced-fat (Neufchâtel) cream cheeses make as rich a frosting as you'll ever taste. This recipe makes enough to fill and frost a 3-layer cake; the orange-flavored variation makes enough to frost a single 8- or 9-inch square or round layer.

12 ounces reduced-fat cream cheese (Neufchâtel), at room temperature
8 ounces nonfat cream cheese, at room temperature
½ cup plain nonfat yogurt
3 cups confectioners' sugar
2 teaspoons vanilla extract

1. In a small bowl, with an electric mixer, beat the reduced-fat and nonfat cream cheeses until smooth.

2. At low speed, beat in the yogurt, confectioners' sugar, and vanilla until smooth and well blended.

VARIATIONS

Lemon-Lime Frosting: Add 1 teaspoon of grated lemon zest and 1 teaspoon of grated lime zest in step 2. Omit the vanilla and replace with 2 teaspoons of lemon juice.
Orange Frosting (for a single-layer cake): Use 4 ounces of reduced-fat cream cheese, 2 ounces of nonfat cream cheese, 2 tablespoons of nonfat yogurt, and 1 cup of confectioners' sugar. Omit the vanilla and use 2 to 3 teaspoons orange juice. Add 1 teaspoon grated orange zest.

Specialty Equipment

Angel food cake pan. This pan has a removable bottom and three feet on which to stand the pan (upside-down) as the cake cools. Angel food cake pans can be used for sponge cakes, too. Our recipe (page 37) calls for a 10-inch pan.

Quiche pan. The fluted ceramic dish used for quiche is also the traditional choice for clafouti (page 147). Although it resembles a tart pan, it shouldn't be used for tarts, which would be tricky to remove from a one-piece pan. Choose a dish with an unglazed bottom for better heat absorption.

Tube pan. This one- or two-piece pan, used for sponge cakes, can also stand in for an angel food cake or Bundt pan. A tube pan that lacks the "feet" usually found on angel food cake pans can be inverted for cooling by resting the edge of the pan on three evenly-spaced glasses or mugs (see page 37). Or slip the tube of the inverted pan over a bottle.

Bundt pan (fluted tube pan). This one-piece tube pan is used for large, dense cakes like pound cakes and, of course, Bundt cakes (see page 26). The cakes turn out tall and attractively fluted. Bundt pans are usually made of cast or stamped aluminum; some have nonstick coatings.

Soufflé dish. An elegant classic, this white porcelain soufflé dish has the straight sides required for a high-rising, puffy soufflé. The dishes come in a wide range of sizes, from petite (for individual soufflés, custards, and puddings) to mammoth (for party main-dish soufflés). Our 4- and 6-serving soufflés (pages 136 and 153) are made in a 1½-quart dish.

Coeur à la crème mold. This specialized piece of equipment is used for making a delicious French summer dessert (see page 138). The heart-shaped dish has a perforated bottom to allow excess liquid to drain off from a sweetened cream-cheese mixture.

Springform pan. The high rim of this two-part pan is a band that can be closed and opened with a clamp; the base and sides fit together tightly. To serve the cake, snap open the rim and remove it, leaving the cake on the base. You'll need a springform pan for making cheesecakes (pages 15 and 35).

Removable-bottom tart pan. This simple design works something like a springform pan, but the rim is one piece. After baking and cooling the tart, stand the pan on a wide-mouth jar or a can and let the rim drop off; leave the tart on the pan's base. We use a 9-inch pan for our tarts (pages 56, 66, and 75).

Tartlet pans. These diminutive versions of the pan above are used for individual pastries such as the tartlets on page 76. Remove the rims by standing each pan on an overturned glass.

CAKES & COOKIES

1

CAPPUCCINO CHEESECAKE

SERVES: 12
WORKING TIME: 20 MINUTES
TOTAL TIME: 2 HOURS 15 MINUTES PLUS CHILLING TIME

While cheesecake may be the original "oh no, there goes my diet" dessert, nobody can blame this cake for dietary downfall. It's made with low-fat cottage cheese and reduced-fat and nonfat cream cheeses, and has only a bottom crust, made with about a quarter the usual quantity of oil. The result: Our rich coffee-infused cake has a fraction of the fat of regular cheesecake.

10 chocolate wafer cookies (about 2½ ounces)

1 tablespoon vegetable oil

1 cup plus 1 tablespoon granulated sugar

3 tablespoons instant espresso powder

3 tablespoons coffee liqueur

1 quart low-fat (1%) cottage cheese

8 ounces reduced-fat cream cheese (Neufchâtel), at room temperature

4 ounces nonfat cream cheese, at room temperature

2 tablespoons flour

2 whole large eggs

2 large egg whites

¼ teaspoon salt

⅛ teaspoon cinnamon

12 chocolate-covered coffee beans (optional)

1. Preheat the oven to 300°. Spray a 9-inch springform pan with nonstick cooking spray. In a food processor, process the chocolate wafers until fine crumbs form. Remove ½ teaspoon of the crumbs and set aside. Add the oil and 1 tablespoon of the sugar and process until the crumbs are evenly moistened. Place the crumb mixture in the prepared pan and press onto the bottom of the pan.

2. In a small bowl, dissolve the espresso powder in the coffee liqueur; set aside. In a food processor, process the cottage cheese until it is very smooth, about 2 minutes. Add the reduced-fat cream cheese, nonfat cream cheese, the remaining 1 cup sugar, the flour, whole eggs, egg whites, salt, cinnamon, and reserved coffee liqueur mixture. Process until smooth.

3. Scrape the batter into the prepared pan and bake for 1 hour and 25 minutes, or until firm around the edges but still wobbly in the center. Turn off the oven and leave the cheesecake in the oven with the door closed for 30 minutes. Transfer to a wire rack to cool completely. Cover and refrigerate until chilled, at least 4 hours. Sprinkle the reserved crumbs around the edge of the cheesecake and decorate with the coffee beans. Remove the springform ring and serve.

Helpful hint: If you don't want to buy a large bottle of coffee liqueur for this recipe, look for the little bottles, called "nips" or "tasters," that are sold in liquor stores; they contain just the amount called for here.

FAT: 7G/27%
CALORIES: 237
SATURATED FAT: 3.1G
CARBOHYDRATE: 28G
PROTEIN: 15G
CHOLESTEROL: 48MG
SODIUM: 534MG

RASPBERRY JAM THUMBPRINTS

MAKES: 3 DOZEN
WORKING TIME: 25 MINUTES
TOTAL TIME: 40 MINUTES PLUS CHILLING AND COOLING TIMES

A lso known as jelly tots or thimble cookies, thumbprint cookies make a good starter recipe when you're teaching children to cook: Kids love to help make the "dimples" and then fill them with jam.

Traditionally these cookies are made with a very rich, buttery dough; here, applesauce takes the place of some of the fat.

1¾ cups flour

½ teaspoon salt

¼ teaspoon baking soda

3 tablespoons unsalted butter

1 tablespoon solid vegetable shortening

3 tablespoons unsweetened applesauce

½ cup granulated sugar

2 teaspoons vanilla extract

1 large egg

2 tablespoons slivered almonds, toasted and finely chopped

¼ cup raspberry jam

1. Preheat the oven to 375°. Spray 2 cookie sheets with nonstick cooking spray. In a medium bowl, combine the flour, salt, and baking soda. In a large bowl, with an electric mixer, beat the butter, shortening, and applesauce until creamy. Blend in the sugar and vanilla. Beat in the egg. Gradually beat in the flour mixture. Cover and refrigerate until chilled, about 30 minutes.

2. Divide the dough into quarters. Divide each quarter into 9 equal pieces. With lightly floured hands, roll each piece of dough into a ball for a total of 36 balls. Spread the almonds on a large plate. Dip one side of each cookie ball into the almonds, pressing gently so the nuts adhere. Place the balls 1 inch apart on the cookie sheets. Make an indentation in the center of each ball with your index finger and fill the indentation with a generous ¼ teaspoon of the jam.

3. Bake the cookies, in 2 batches, for 9 to 11 minutes, or until the cookies are just barely colored on the bottom. Transfer to a wire rack and serve when cool.

Helpful hints: Raspberry jam is just one possibility for filling these cookies: Strawberry or cherry jam, or orange marmalade, are other good choices. To toast almonds (or any nuts), spread them out in a small baking pan and bake them in a 350° oven for 8 to 10 minutes, shaking the pan occasionally to keep them from scorching.

VALUES ARE PER COOKIE
FAT: 2G/29%
CALORIES: 56
SATURATED FAT: 0.7G
CARBOHYDRATE: 9G
PROTEIN: 1G
CHOLESTEROL: 9MG
SODIUM: 42MG

BLONDIES

MAKES: 12 BLONDIES
WORKING TIME: 15 MINUTES
TOTAL TIME: 55 MINUTES PLUS COOLING TIME

½ cup pitted prunes
1 cup flour
½ teaspoon baking soda
¼ teaspoon salt
¾ cup firmly packed light brown sugar
¼ cup vegetable oil
1 large egg
3 tablespoons light corn syrup
1 teaspoon vanilla extract
1 tablespoons pecans, toasted and chopped

1. Preheat the oven to 350°. Spray a 9-inch square baking pan with nonstick cooking spray and line the bottom with waxed paper. Spray the paper with nonstick cooking spray.

2. In a food processor, combine the prunes and 2 tablespoons of water and process until smooth; set aside.

3. On a sheet of waxed paper, sift together the flour, baking soda, and salt. In a large bowl, combine the brown sugar, oil, prune purée, egg, corn syrup, and vanilla. Add the flour mixture, stirring until well combined. Scrape into the prepared pan, sprinkle the nuts over, and bake until a toothpick inserted in the center comes out just clean, about 20 to 25 minutes. Cool in the pan on a wire rack before cutting and serving.

Helpful hints: You can substitute walnuts or peanuts for the pecans if you like. To toast the pecans (or any nuts), spread them out in a small baking pan and bake them in a 350° oven for 8 to 10 minutes, shaking the pan occasionally to keep them from scorching.

VALUES ARE PER BLONDIE
FAT: 6G/29%
CALORIES: 172
SATURATED FAT: 0.7G
CARBOHYDRATE: 32G
PROTEIN: 2G
CHOLESTEROL: 18MG
SODIUM: 115MG

Blondies are also called blond brownies—they're the "unchocolate" version of those delicious, chewy bar cookies. We've made a major dent in the fat content of traditional blondies. Instead of a stick of butter, we've used a small amount of vegetable oil plus a prune purée that mimics the function of fat in baked goods.

The most unlikely "pie" you'll ever eat, Boston Cream Pie is actually two layers of cake filled with custardy pastry cream. Topped with chocolate frosting, this version is similar to "Parker House chocolate pie," named for the famous Boston hotel. Surprisingly, our lush frosting is made without any butter at all.

BOSTON CREAM PIE

Serves: 10
Working time: 40 minutes
Total time: 1 hour 5 minutes plus cooling time

Vanilla Pastry Cream (p. 10)

1¼ cups cake flour

¾ teaspoon baking powder

¼ teaspoon baking soda

⅛ teaspoon salt

1 whole large egg

1 large egg white

3 tablespoons unsalted butter, at room temperature

¾ cup plus 1 tablespoon granulated sugar

¾ cup low-fat (1.5%) buttermilk

2 tablespoons light corn syrup

1 tablespoon low-fat (1%) milk

3½ ounces chocolate chips (about 7 tablespoons)

2 tablespoons unsweetened cocoa powder

½ teaspoon vanilla extract

1. Make the pastry cream, transfer to a bowl, place plastic wrap directly on the surface, and refrigerate while you make the cake. Preheat the oven to 350°. Spray two 8-inch cake pans with non-stick cooking spray. Dust with flour, shaking off the excess.

2. On a sheet of waxed paper, sift together the flour, baking powder, baking soda, and salt. In a small bowl, whisk together the whole egg and egg white. In a large bowl, with an electric mixer, beat the butter and ¾ cup of the sugar until creamy. Gradually beat in the egg mixture, 1 teaspoon at a time, until light in texture. With a rubber spatula, alternately fold in the flour mixture and buttermilk, beginning and ending with the flour mixture, until just blended. Scrape into the prepared pans and bake for 15 to 20 minutes, or until a toothpick inserted in the center comes out clean. Cool the cakes in the pans on wire racks for 5 minutes. Turn out onto the racks to cool completely.

3. Meanwhile, in a small saucepan, combine the corn syrup, the remaining 1 tablespoon sugar, and the milk and heat over low heat, stirring occasionally, until the sugar dissolves. Stir in the chocolate chips, cocoa, and 2 tablespoons of water and cook until the chocolate is melted and the mixture is smooth. Remove from the heat and whisk in the vanilla. Assemble the cake as directed in the tip at right.

Fat: 9g/29%
Calories: 281
Saturated Fat: 4.9g
Carbohydrate: 47g
Protein: 5g
Cholesterol: 56mg
Sodium: 142mg

Lemon Layer Cake with Lemon-Lime Frosting

SERVES: 16
WORKING TIME: 50 MINUTES
TOTAL TIME: 1 HOUR 10 MINUTES PLUS COOLING TIME

Layer cakes are for special occasions, and triple-layer cakes are for the most special of all—birthdays and anniversaries, engagement parties, college graduations. You can ice the cake with a lavish hand and a clear conscience, knowing that the frosting is made with reduced-fat and nonfat cream cheese instead of butter.

2 cups flour
1 teaspoon baking soda
½ cup unsalted butter, at room temperature
2 cups granulated sugar
2 large egg yolks
1 cup low-fat (1.5%) buttermilk
2 tablespoons fresh lemon juice
1 teaspoon grated lemon zest
1 teaspoon vanilla extract
6 large egg whites, at room temperature
Lemon-Lime Cream Cheese Frosting (p. 11)
3 tablespoons slivered lemon zest
3 tablespoons slivered lime zest

1. Preheat the oven to 350°. Spray three 8-inch round cake pans with nonstick cooking spray, line the bottoms with waxed paper, and spray again. Dust with flour, shaking off the excess. In a small bowl, combine the 2 cups flour and baking soda. In a large bowl, with an electric mixer, beat the butter and 1 cup of the sugar until creamy. Add the egg yolks, one at a time, beating well after each addition. Alternately beat in the flour mixture and the buttermilk, beginning and ending with the flour mixture. Beat in the lemon juice, the grated lemon zest, and the vanilla.

2. In a separate mixing bowl, with clean beaters, beat the egg whites until stiff peaks form. Gradually beat in the remaining 1 cup sugar. Fold the egg whites into the batter and scrape the batter into the prepared pans, smoothing the tops. Bake for 20 to 23 minutes, or until a toothpick inserted in the center comes out clean. Cool the cakes in the pans on wire racks for 5 minutes. Turn the cakes out onto the racks to cool completely. Make the frosting.

3. Place one cake layer on a serving plate. Spread with 1 cup of the frosting. Top with another cake layer and another 1 cup frosting. Top with the third layer and spread the remaining frosting over the top and sides of the cake. In a small bowl, combine the slivered lemon and lime zests. Gently toss the zest over the top and onto the sides of the cake and serve.

FAT: 10G/24%
CALORIES: 381
SATURATED FAT: 6.3G
CARBOHYDRATE: 64G
PROTEIN: 8G
CHOLESTEROL: 55MG
SODIUM: 282MG

MONSTER COOKIES

MAKES: 8 COOKIES
WORKING TIME: 25 MINUTES
TOTAL TIME: 45 MINUTES PLUS COOLING TIME

The saucer-sized "black-and-white" is a New York City classic—woe to the bakery that runs out of this perennial favorite! Like sandwich cookies, black-and-whites inspire various eating styles (first one side, then the other, or a bite of chocolate, then one of vanilla). However they're eaten, these chocolate chip "monster" cookies should please everyone.

1⅔ cups flour
½ teaspoon baking powder
½ teaspoon baking soda
½ teaspoon cinnamon
¼ teaspoon salt
⅓ cup reduced-fat sour cream
¼ cup unsalted butter
⅔ cup granulated sugar
¼ cup plus 1 teaspoon light corn syrup
¼ cup raisins
2 ounces mini chocolate chips (about ¼ cup)
2 teaspoons unsweetened cocoa powder
Vanilla Sugar Glaze or Orange Glaze (p. 11)

1. Preheat the oven to 350°. On a sheet of waxed paper, sift together the flour, baking powder, baking soda, cinnamon, and salt. In a large bowl, beat the sour cream and butter until creamy. Add the sugar and ¼ cup of the corn syrup and beat until light and fluffy. Fold in the flour mixture just until combined. Fold in the raisins and 2 tablespoons of the chocolate chips.

2. Line 2 baking sheets with parchment paper (or spray with nonstick cooking spray). Place the dough by scant ⅓ cupfuls 3 inches apart on the prepared baking sheets for a total of 8 cookies. Flatten each to a 4-inch round. Bake for 20 minutes, reversing the sheets in the oven halfway through, until the cookies are lightly golden and just set. Transfer to a wire rack to cool.

3. In a small bowl set in a pan of hot water, melt together the remaining 2 tablespoons chocolate chips, the remaining 1 teaspoon corn syrup, the cocoa, and 1 tablespoon of water. Stir until the icing is of a spreading consistency. Spread the chocolate icing over half of each cookie. Make the sugar glaze, spread over the other half, and serve.

Helpful hint: To delight children on Halloween, use 1 or 2 drops of food coloring to tint the white frosting a pale orange.

VALUES ARE PER COOKIE
FAT: 9G/22%
CALORIES: 368
SATURATED FAT: 5.5G
CARBOHYDRATE: 70G
PROTEIN: 4G
CHOLESTEROL: 19MG
SODIUM: 199MG

CHOCOLATE-ORANGE BUNDT CAKE

SERVES: 16
WORKING TIME: 20 MINUTES
TOTAL TIME: 1 HOUR 5 MINUTES PLUS COOLING TIME

3 cups cake flour
⅔ cup unsweetened cocoa
powder
2 teaspoons baking powder
1 teaspoon baking soda
½ teaspoon salt
1 cup pitted prunes
⅓ cup hot water
2 large eggs
2 cups granulated sugar
½ cup vegetable oil
4 teaspoons grated orange zest
2 teaspoons instant coffee
granules
2 teaspoons vanilla extract
2 cups low-fat (1.5%)
buttermilk
Orange Drizzle (p. 11)

1. Preheat oven to 350°. Spray a 12-cup Bundt pan with nonstick cooking spray. On a sheet of waxed paper, sift together the flour, cocoa powder, baking powder, baking soda, and salt; set aside.

2. In a food processor, process the prunes and hot water to a smooth purée. Transfer the mixture to a large bowl and add the eggs, sugar, oil, orange zest, coffee granules, and vanilla. With an electric mixer, beat the mixture until well blended. Alternately fold in the flour mixture and the buttermilk, beginning and ending with the flour mixture, until just combined.

3. Scrape the batter into the prepared pan and smooth the top. Bake for 1 hour and 5 minutes, or until the top of the cake springs back when touched lightly and a toothpick inserted halfway between the sides and the center tube comes out clean. Cool the cake in the pan on a rack for 15 minutes. Turn out of the pan onto the rack to cool completely. Make the orange drizzle. Place the cake on a serving plate, spoon the orange drizzle over the top, letting it drip down the sides, and serve.

Helpful hint: If the drizzle is too thick, add more liquid (orange juice or water) ½ teaspoon at a time. You can spoon the glaze into a small plastic bag, then snip off the very tip of one corner of the bag. You'll then be able to "pipe" the glaze neatly onto the cake.

FAT: 9G/25%
CALORIES: 331
SATURATED FAT: 1.7G
CARBOHYDRATE: 62G
PROTEIN: 5G
CHOLESTEROL: 28MG
SODIUM: 234MG

A crownlike Bundt cake is prettiest when its fluted shape is highlighted with a contrasting glaze. A fine example is our tall, dark, and handsome chocolate cake silhouetted with an orange-flavored white "drizzle." The fat-saving secret in this recipe is prune purée (made in seconds in the food processor): It stands in for part of the shortening.

CARROT CAKE

SERVES: 12
WORKING TIME: 30 MINUTES
TOTAL TIME: 1 HOUR 20 MINUTES PLUS COOLING TIME

There was doubtless a healthy impulse behind the first carrot cake, but nowadays it's hard to find a recipe for one that doesn't call for tons of oil (or butter) and a pound of cream cheese. This, however, is a carrot cake to feel good about: It's made in a single layer with a small amount of oil. After baking, it's topped with a zesty reduced-fat cream cheese icing, and it's delicious.

2 cups flour
2 teaspoons cinnamon
1½ teaspoons baking soda
½ teaspoon salt
½ teaspoon ground ginger
⅛ teaspoon ground cloves
⅛ teaspoon nutmeg
½ cup unsweetened applesauce
½ cup firmly packed light brown sugar
½ cup orange juice
¼ cup vegetable oil
1 whole large egg
1 large egg white
1½ cups grated carrots
⅓ cup raisins
¼ cup canned juice-packed crushed pineapple, drained
1½ teaspoons vanilla extract
Orange Cream Cheese Frosting (p. 11)

1. Preheat the oven to 325°. Spray a 9-inch square baking pan with nonstick cooking spray.

2. In a medium bowl, combine the flour, cinnamon, baking soda, salt, ginger, cloves, and nutmeg; set aside. In a large bowl, combine the applesauce, brown sugar, orange juice, oil, whole egg, and egg white, whisking until well combined. Stir in the carrots, raisins, pineapple, and vanilla. Fold in the flour mixture.

3. Scrape the batter into the prepared pan and smooth the top. Bake for 45 to 50 minutes, or until a toothpick inserted in the center comes out clean. Cool in the pan on a wire rack for 10 minutes. Turn the cake out onto the rack to cool completely.

4. Meanwhile, make the orange frosting. Place the cooled cake on a plate, spread the frosting on top, and serve.

Helpful hint: For a whimsical garnish, top each piece of cake with a carrot curl (made with a vegetable peeler) and a mint sprig.

FAT: 7G/24%
CALORIES: 258
SATURATED FAT: 1.8G
CARBOHYDRATE: 44G
PROTEIN: 5G
CHOLESTEROL: 23MG
SODIUM: 337MG

GLAZED RASPBERRY-FUDGE CAKE

SERVES: 12
WORKING TIME: 45 MINUTES
TOTAL TIME: 1 HOUR 15 MINUTES PLUS COOLING TIME

This towering, fudgy cake is a party in itself served with strong coffee, fragrant tea, or tall glasses of icy-cold milk. We've "gilded the lily" a bit with raspberries and quill-like chocolate curls, made by peeling shavings from a thick bar of chocolate; this can be done with a vegetable peeler or a large chef's knife when the chocolate is at room temperature.

½ cup plus ⅓ cup unsweetened cocoa powder, plus extra for dusting

2¼ cups cake flour

2 teaspoons baking soda

¼ teaspoon salt

¼ cup unsalted butter, at room temperature

2¼ cups firmly packed light brown sugar

1 whole large egg

2 large egg whites

1 cup nonfat sour cream

1 ounce unsweetened chocolate, melted and cooled

3 teaspoons vanilla extract

1 cup boiling water

1½ cups seedless raspberry jam

1 ounce chocolate chips (about 2 tablespoons)

1. Preheat the oven to 350°. Spray three 8-inch round cake pans with nonstick cooking spray, line the bottoms with waxed paper, and spray again. Dust with cocoa powder, shaking off the excess.

2. On a sheet of waxed paper, sift together the flour, ½ cup of the cocoa, the baking soda, and salt. In a large bowl, with an electric mixer, beat the butter and brown sugar until creamy. Beat in the whole egg and egg whites, one at a time, beating well after each addition. Beat in the sour cream. Stir in the melted chocolate and 1 teaspoon of the vanilla. Alternately beat in the flour mixture and the boiling water in thirds, beginning and ending with the flour. Divide the batter evenly among the cake pans. Bake for 25 minutes, or until the cake is beginning to pull away from the sides of the pans. Do not overbake. Set on wire racks to cool completely.

3. Meanwhile, in a small saucepan, combine the remaining ⅓ cup cocoa, ½ cup of the jam, the chocolate chips, and 1 tablespoon of water. Bring to a boil over low heat, stirring, and cook until smooth, about 1 minute. Remove from the heat and stir in the remaining 2 teaspoons vanilla. Set aside to cool for 30 minutes.

4. Spread a cake layer with ½ cup of the jam. Top with a second cake layer and coat with the remaining ½ cup jam. Top with the third layer and pour the fudge glaze on top, letting it drip down the sides. Let the cake rest at least 15 minutes before serving.

FAT: 8G/17%
CALORIES: 428
SATURATED FAT: 4.3G
CARBOHYDRATE: 89G
PROTEIN: 6G
CHOLESTEROL: 29MG
SODIUM: 318MG

GINGERSNAPS

MAKES: 5 DOZEN
WORKING TIME: 15 MINUTES
TOTAL TIME: 30 MINUTES PLUS CHILLING AND COOLING TIME

These striped icebox cookies are spiced with ginger, cinnamon, and cloves, and are topped with a sweet and tangy lemon-ginger icing.

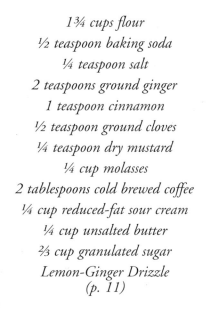

1¾ cups flour
½ teaspoon baking soda
¼ teaspoon salt
2 teaspoons ground ginger
1 teaspoon cinnamon
½ teaspoon ground cloves
¼ teaspoon dry mustard
¼ cup molasses
2 tablespoons cold brewed coffee
¼ cup reduced-fat sour cream
¼ cup unsalted butter
⅔ cup granulated sugar
Lemon-Ginger Drizzle
(p. 11)

1. In a medium bowl, sift together the flour, baking soda, and salt. Stir in the ginger, cinnamon, cloves, and mustard until well combined. In a small bowl, combine the molasses and coffee. In a large bowl, with an electric mixer, beat together the sour cream and butter until creamy. Add the sugar and beat until light and fluffy. Alternately beat in the flour mixture and the molasses mixture, beginning and ending with the flour mixture, until just combined.

2. Halve the dough and shape each half into a log about 7 inches long and 1 inch wide. Wrap the logs well in waxed paper and freeze for 45 minutes or refrigerate for several hours, until firm.

3. Preheat the oven to 350°. Line 2 cookie sheets with parchment paper (or spray with nonstick cooking spray). Slice the cookies a scant ¼ inch thick and place 1 inch apart on the cookie sheets. Bake the cookies, 1 sheet at a time, for 8 minutes, or until the cookies are no longer shiny and are just set. Transfer to a wire rack to cool. Repeat until all of the dough is used. Meanwhile, make the lemon-ginger drizzle. Drizzle the icing over the cooled cookies and serve.

Helpful hint: Fat acts as a preservative in baked goods, so these low-fat cookies harden rather quickly; they're best eaten the day they're baked. However, the dough can be frozen for up to a month.

VALUES ARE PER COOKIE
FAT: 1G/21%
CALORIES: 42
SATURATED FAT: 0.5G
CARBOHYDRATE: 8G
PROTEIN: 0.4G
CHOLESTEROL: 2MG
SODIUM: 21MG

BROWNIES

MAKES: 16 BROWNIES
WORKING TIME: 15 MINUTES
TOTAL TIME: 50 MINUTES PLUS COOLING TIME

1 cup pitted prunes

⅓ cup hot water

¾ cup flour

¾ cup plus 2 tablespoons firmly packed light brown sugar

⅓ cup unsweetened cocoa powder

¾ teaspoon baking powder

⅛ teaspoon salt

¼ cup vegetable oil

2 ounces chocolate chips (about ¼ cup), melted and cooled

¼ cup light corn syrup

1 whole large egg

1 large egg white

2 teaspoons vanilla extract

1 tablespoon plus 1½ teaspoons chopped walnuts

1. Preheat the oven to 350°. Spray an 8-inch square baking pan with nonstick cooking spray. Line the bottom with waxed paper. In a food processor, process the prunes and hot water to a smooth purée.

2. In a large bowl, combine the flour, brown sugar, cocoa powder, baking powder, salt, oil, melted chocolate, corn syrup, whole egg, and egg white. Stir in the prune purée and vanilla.

3. Scrape the batter into the prepared pan and smooth the top. Sprinkle the walnuts over and bake for about 35 minutes, or until a toothpick inserted in the center comes out clean. Cool the brownies in the pan on a wire rack before cutting and serving.

Helpful hint: If you want to freeze the brownies, turn out the whole uncut "cake" onto a sheet of foil, wrap, and freeze: They'll stay fresher if you don't cut them until you're ready to serve.

VALUES ARE PER BROWNIE
FAT: 6G/29%
CALORIES: 170
SATURATED FAT: 1.3G
CARBOHYDRATE: 31G
PROTEIN: 2G
CHOLESTEROL: 13MG
SODIUM: 59MG

Good news! America's favorite bar cookie has been slimmed down— with no loss of fudgy flavor.

CREAMY ORANGE CHEESECAKE

SERVES: 12
WORKING TIME: 25 MINUTES
TOTAL TIME: 1 HOUR 25 MINUTES PLUS CHILLING TIME

Cheesecake can be a weighty affair in more ways than one: Some recipes call for as much as two and a half pounds of cream cheese, which add up to 400 grams of fat—and that's not counting the butter, cream, and egg yolks.

A combination of nonfat cottage cheese and Neufchâtel (reduced-fat cream cheese) gives this citrusy cake a lovely texture with just a fraction of the fat.

Chocolate-Graham Cookie Crust (p. 10)
2½ cups nonfat cottage cheese
12 ounces reduced-fat cream cheese (Neufchâtel)
1½ cups granulated sugar
1½ cups nonfat sour cream
½ cup frozen orange juice concentrated, thawed
⅓ cup nonfat dry milk powder
2 whole large eggs
3 large egg whites
2 teaspoons vanilla extract
¼ teaspoon salt

1. Preheat the oven to 325°. Prepare the crust through step 1. Measure out 1 tablespoon of the crust mixture and set aside. Scrape the remaining crust mixture into a 9-inch springform pan and press it onto the bottom and 1 inch up the sides of the pan. Set aside.

2. In a blender or food processor, process the cottage cheese and cream cheese until very smooth. Add the sugar, sour cream, orange juice concentrate, milk powder, whole eggs, egg whites, vanilla, and salt. Process until well combined.

3. Pour the filling into the crust and bake for 55 to 65 minutes, or until the center of the cheesecake is slightly jiggly, the edges start to brown, and the cake is puffed. Set on a wire rack to cool for 1 hour. Cover tightly and refrigerate until well chilled, at least 4 hours. Sprinkle the reserved crust mixture over the cake and remove the springform ring. Using a sharp knife, cut the cake, wetting the knife before each slice, and serve.

Helpful hint: To make the garnish shown in the photograph, cut a thin slice of orange and notch it from the center to one edge; then twist the slice as shown. The cake could also be garnished with knots or bows made from strips of orange zest.

FAT: 9G/22%
CALORIES: 376
SATURATED FAT: 4.2G
CARBOHYDRATE: 57G
PROTEIN: 15G
CHOLESTEROL: 53MG
SODIUM: 530MG

Angel food cake has a long, lean history: The basic recipe for this airy cake has been around for more than 100 years, and it's always been free of both shortening and egg yolks. Our version is flecked with chocolate and served in a pool of strawberry-orange sauce. For a graceful finishing touch, garnish the cake with fresh strawberries and orange twists.

CHOCOLATE CHIP ANGEL FOOD CAKE

SERVES: 8
WORKING TIME: 30 MINUTES
TOTAL TIME: 1 HOUR 30 MINUTES PLUS COOLING TIME

1 cup sifted cake flour

1⅓ cups granulated sugar

6 ounces mini chocolate chips (about ¾ cup)

12 large egg whites, at room temperature

1 teaspoon cream of tartar

¼ teaspoon salt

1 tablespoon fresh lemon juice

1½ teaspoons vanilla extract

¼ teaspoon almond extract

2 teaspoons confectioners' sugar

12-ounce package frozen unsweetened strawberries or raspberries

¼ cup orange juice

2 tablespoons strawberry or raspberry jam

1. Preheat the oven to 350". On a sheet of waxed paper, sift together the flour and ⅓ cup of the sugar; set aside. In a small bowl, toss 2 tablespoons of the flour mixture with the chocolate chips and set aside.

2. In a large bowl, with an electric mixer, beat the egg whites, cream of tartar, and salt until soft peaks form. Gradually beat in the remaining 1 cup sugar, 1 tablespoon at a time, until very stiff peaks form. Beat in the lemon juice, vanilla extract, and almond extract, beating until well combined.

3. Sift the flour-sugar mixture over the egg white mixture and sprinkle the chocolate chips lightly over the top. Fold the flour mixture and chocolate chips into the egg whites. Pour the batter into an ungreased 10-inch angel food cake pan or tube pan and bake for 1 hour, or until the cake is golden brown and pulls away from the sides of the pan. Cool the cake upside down in the pan (see tip). Then loosen the sides with a metal spatula and invert onto a cake plate. Using a fine-mesh sieve, dust the cake with the confectioners' sugar.

4. Meanwhile, in a food processor, combine the strawberries, orange juice, and jam and process to a smooth purée. Spoon the strawberry sauce onto 8 plates. With a serrated knife, cut the cake and serve over the sauce.

FAT: 6G/16%
CALORIES: 334
SATURATED FAT: 3.4G
CARBOHYDRATE: 66G
PROTEIN: 7G
CHOLESTEROL: 0MG
SODIUM: 154MG

TIP

Like all angel food cakes, this cake cools upside down so it doesn't become compact. If you don't have a true angel food cake pan, which has legs to support it while it cools, you can fashion a cooling rack that will allow the cake to be suspended: Invert three glasses of the same height on a flat surface, using the cake pan to space them so the rim of the pan just rests on them.

OATMEAL COOKIES

MAKES: 2 DOZEN
WORKING TIME: 25 MINUTES
TOTAL TIME: 1 HOUR PLUS COOLING TIME

The cookie jar won't stay full for long, once you fill it with these hefty oatmeal-fruit cookies. Applesauce in the dough lets you use less butter, and it helps keep the cookies moist. The dried cherries we've included are fairly new on the market; if your local stores don't carry them, substitute raisins or snipped dried apricots.

2 cups old-fashioned rolled oats
1¼ cups flour
1 teaspoon baking soda
1 teaspoon cinnamon
½ teaspoon salt
½ cup regular (sweetened) applesauce
½ cup firmly packed light brown sugar
¼ cup plus 2 tablespoons granulated sugar
¼ cup unsalted butter, at room temperature
1 large egg
½ cup low-fat (1%) milk
1 teaspoon vanilla extract
1 cup dried cherries

1. Preheat the oven to 375°. Spread the oats in a jelly-roll pan and toast, stirring occasionally, for 7 to 10 minutes, or until lightly browned. Leave the oven on. Spray 2 cookie sheets with nonstick cooking spray.

2. In a medium bowl, combine the oats, flour, baking soda, cinnamon, and salt. In a large bowl, whisk together the applesauce, brown sugar, ¼ cup of the granulated sugar, the butter, egg, milk, and vanilla. With a wooden spoon, stir the oat mixture into the applesauce mixture until blended. Stir in the dried cherries.

3. Drop the dough by rounded tablespoons 2 inches apart on the prepared baking sheets. With the bottom of a glass, flatten each cookie to make a 2-inch round. Sprinkle the cookies with the remaining 2 tablespoons sugar. Bake the cookies, in 2 batches, for 10 to 15 minutes, or until lightly browned. Transfer to wire racks to cool completely before serving.

Helpful hint: To prevent the glass from sticking when you flatten the balls of dough, coat the bottom of the glass with granulated sugar. Dip the glass in water, then into a saucer of sugar. After you've flattened the first cookie, the glass will become sticky and the sugar will adhere to it.

VALUES ARE PER COOKIE
FAT: 3G/22%
CALORIES: 121
SATURATED FAT: 1.4G
CARBOHYDRATE: 23G
PROTEIN: 2G
CHOLESTEROL: 14MG
SODIUM: 106MG

DOUBLE CHOCOLATE CHEWS

MAKES: 2 DOZEN
WORKING TIME: 20 MINUTES
TOTAL TIME: 30 MINUTES PLUS COOLING TIME

*I*t

may be hard to believe, but both "double chocolate" and "low in fat" are phrases that describe this big, beautiful cookie.

1 cup flour

½ cup unsweetened cocoa powder

¼ teaspoon salt

3 tablespoons unsalted butter

2½ ounces nonfat cream cheese

⅓ cup granulated sugar

½ cup firmly packed dark brown sugar

1 teaspoon vanilla extract

1½ ounces mini chocolate chips (about 3 tablespoons)

1. Preheat the oven to 350°. Spray 2 cookie sheets with nonstick cooking spray.

2. On a sheet of waxed paper, sift together the flour, cocoa powder, and salt. In a large bowl, with an electric mixer, beat the butter, cream cheese, granulated sugar, and brown sugar until creamy. Beat in the vanilla. Beat the flour mixture into the butter mixture. With your fingers, knead in the chocolate chips.

3. Divide the dough into quarters. Divide each quarter into 6 equal pieces. Roll each piece of dough into a ball and place on the prepared cookie sheets. Repeat to form 24 balls. Using the bottom of a glass, press the balls into 2-inch rounds.

4. Bake the cookies, in two batches, for 8 minutes, or until slightly puffed and very soft to the touch. Let cool on the pans for 1 minute, then transfer to wire racks to cool before serving.

Helpful hint: To prevent the glass from sticking when you flatten the balls of dough, coat the bottom of the glass with granulated sugar. Dip the glass in water, then into a saucer of sugar. After you've flattened the first cookie, the glass will become sticky and the sugar will adhere to it.

VALUES ARE PER COOKIE
FAT: 2G/24%
CALORIES: 76
SATURATED FAT: 1.3G
CARBOHYDRATE: 14G
PROTEIN: 1G
CHOLESTEROL: 4MG
SODIUM: 39MG

Zesty Lemon Squares

MAKES: 16 SQUARES
WORKING TIME: 15 MINUTES
TOTAL TIME: 1 HOUR 20 MINUTES PLUS COOLING TIME

¼ cup unsalted butter

2 ounces nonfat cream cheese

1¼ cups granulated sugar

¾ cup plus 3 tablespoons flour

¼ teaspoon salt

1 whole large egg

3 large egg whites

1 tablespoon grated lemon zest

¼ cup plus 2 tablespoons fresh
lemon juice

½ teaspoon baking powder

1 teaspoon confectioners' sugar

1. Preheat the oven to 350°. In a medium bowl, with an electric mixer, beat the butter, cream cheese, and ¼ cup of the granulated sugar until creamy. Blend in ¾ cup of the flour and the salt on low speed until the mixture resembles fine crumbs. Press the mixture evenly over the bottom of an 8-inch square baking pan. Bake for 20 minutes.

2. Meanwhile, in a medium bowl, with an electric mixer, beat the whole egg, egg whites, and remaining 1 cup granulated sugar until thick, about 2 minutes. Beat in the lemon zest, lemon juice, remaining 3 tablespoons flour, and the baking powder and beat for 2 minutes.

3. Pour the filling over the baked crust and return to the oven for about 25 minutes, or until the topping is firm in the center and golden brown around the edges. Cool in the pan on a wire rack. Cut into 2-inch squares and transfer to a plate. Just before serving, dust with the confectioners' sugar.

Helpful hints: The crust for these cookies (step 1) can be baked up to a day in advance and kept covered in the refrigerator until you're ready to use it. You'll need 2 medium lemons for the 6 tablespoons of juice called for.

VALUES ARE PER SQUARE
FAT: 3G/21%
CALORIES: 126
SATURATED FAT: 1.9G
CARBOHYDRATE: 22G
PROTEIN: 2G
CHOLESTEROL: 21MG
SODIUM: 81MG

These delicate lemon bars are perfect for afternoon tea. We've cut half a stick of butter from the classic recipe.

41

Raspberry-Filled Chocolate Cupcakes

MAKES: 1 DOZEN
WORKING TIME: 30 MINUTES
TOTAL TIME: 50 MINUTES PLUS COOLING TIME

The cream-filled cupcakes of our childhoods now have a grown-up counterpart: petite chocolate cakes with hearts of raspberry jam (which you can flavor with raspberry liqueur for a truly adult treat).

The cupcakes are decorated with a swirl of semisweet chocolate and a few fresh berries. Red paper cups add a note of sophistication; look for them in kitchenware shops.

⅓ cup raspberry spreadable fruit

¾ teaspoon raspberry-flavored liqueur (optional)

1¼ cups flour

3 tablespoons unsweetened cocoa powder

½ teaspoon baking soda

⅛ teaspoon salt

¼ cup unsalted butter, at room temperature

½ cup granulated sugar

1 large egg

⅔ cup low-fat (1%) milk

½ ounce chocolate chips (about 1 tablespoon), melted

1 cup fresh raspberries

1. Preheat the oven to 375°. Line twelve 2½-inch muffin-tin cups with paper liners or spray with nonstick cooking spray; set aside. In a small bowl, combine the raspberry spreadable fruit and the raspberry liqueur; set aside.

2. In a medium bowl, combine the flour, cocoa powder, baking soda, and salt. In a large bowl, with an electric mixer, beat the butter and sugar until light and fluffy. Add the egg and beat until well combined. Alternately beat in the flour mixture and the milk, beginning and ending with the flour mixture.

3. Spoon about 1 tablespoon of batter into each muffin cup. Make a small indentation in the batter. Dividing evenly, spoon the raspberry spreadable fruit mixture into each indentation (using about 1¼ teaspoon per cupcake). Spoon the remaining batter evenly over the raspberry mixture. Bake for 20 minutes, or until the tops of the cupcakes spring back when lightly touched. Turn the cupcakes out onto a wire rack to cool completely.

4. Spoon the melted chocolate into a small plastic bag, then snip off the very tip of one corner of the bag. Pipe the melted chocolate on top of each cupcake. Top with fresh raspberries before serving.

Helpful hint: If you like, cherry-flavored kirsch can be substituted for the raspberry-flavored liqueur.

VALUES ARE PER CUPCAKE
FAT: 5G/29%
CALORIES: 158
SATURATED FAT: 2.9G
CARBOHYDRATE: 26G
PROTEIN: 3G
CHOLESTEROL: 29MG
SODIUM: 89MG

*T*hough only a modest amount of butter is used in this cake, the buttery flavor is quite prominent. That's because the top of the cake is glazed with a mixture of butter and brown sugar (these ingredients go into the pan first, so they end up as a topping when the cake is turned out). Be sure to try a slice of this cake while it's still warm.

44

PINEAPPLE UPSIDE-DOWN CAKE

SERVES: 12
WORKING TIME: 25 MINUTES
TOTAL TIME: 1 HOUR 20 MINUTES PLUS COOLING TIME

¼ cup plus 1 tablespoon unsalted butter

½ cup firmly packed light brown sugar

Two 8-ounce cans juice-packed pineapple rings, drained and juice reserved

8 dried cherries or raisins

2¼ cups sifted cake flour

2½ teaspoons baking powder

½ teaspoon baking soda

¼ teaspoon salt

¼ cup reduced-fat sour cream

1 cup granulated sugar

1 whole large egg

4 large egg whites

2 teaspoons vanilla extract

⅔ cup low-fat (1%) milk

1. Preheat the oven to 325°. In a 10-inch ovenproof skillet, preferably cast iron, melt 1 tablespoon of the butter over low heat. Stir in the brown sugar and 2 tablespoons of the reserved pineapple juice. Cook until the sugar is dissolved and the mixture is smooth, about 1 minute. Remove from the heat. Arrange the pineapple rings in a single layer on top of the brown sugar mixture. Place a dried cherry in the center of each pineapple ring; set aside.

2. On a sheet of waxed paper, sift together the flour, baking powder, baking soda, and salt. In a large bowl, with an electric mixer, beat the remaining ¼ cup butter, the sour cream, and sugar until light and fluffy. Beat in the whole egg and egg whites, one at a time, beating well after each addition. Beat in the vanilla. With a wooden spoon, alternately stir in the flour mixture and the milk, beginning and ending with the flour mixture, until just combined.

3. Carefully spoon the batter over the pineapple slices. Bake for 50 to 55 minutes, or until a toothpick inserted in the center comes out clean. Transfer to a wire rack and cool the cake in the skillet for 5 minutes. Run a knife around the edges of the skillet and invert the cake onto a heatproof plate (see tip).

Helpful hint: If your skillet doesn't have an ovenproof handle, wrap the handle in a double thickness of foil so that it does not scorch.

FAT: 6G/21%
CALORIES: 260
SATURATED FAT: 3.5G
CARBOHYDRATE: 48G
PROTEIN: 4G
CHOLESTEROL: 33MG
SODIUM: 237MG

TIP

When the cake has cooled slightly, place a heatproof serving plate over the skillet, then invert the skillet and plate. Then carefully lift the skillet; the cake should slip out onto the plate.

CHOCOLATE-HAZELNUT BISCOTTI

MAKES: 4 DOZEN
WORKING TIME: 35 MINUTES
TOTAL TIME: 1 HOUR 5 MINUTES PLUS COOLING TIME

Two trips into the oven— that's the distinguishing feature of biscotti and the source of their name (biscotti means "twice baked" in Italian). The dough is formed into a flattened log for the first baking, then sliced into thick cookies for the second. Crisp and never too sweet, biscotti are intended for dipping— into coffee, tea, cocoa, or milk. Italians like to dip them into sweet wine.

⅓ cup hazelnuts
2⅓ cups flour
1¾ teaspoons baking powder
¼ teaspoon salt
2 tablespoons unsalted butter, at room temperature
1 cup granulated sugar
¼ cup unsweetened cocoa powder
1 whole large egg
1 large egg white
1 teaspoon grated orange zest
2 tablespoons orange juice
1 teaspoon vanilla extract

1. Preheat the oven to 375°. Spray a baking sheet with nonstick cooking spray; set aside. Place the hazelnuts in a baking pan and toast for 7 to 10 minutes, or until the nuts are lightly browned. Leave the oven on. When cool enough to handle, place the hazelnuts in a kitchen towel and and rub the hazelnuts together to loosen the skin (not all of the skin will come off). Finely chop the nuts.

2. In a medium bowl, combine the chopped nuts, the flour, baking powder, and salt; set aside. In a large bowl, with an electric mixer, combine the butter, sugar, cocoa powder, whole egg, egg white, orange zest, orange juice, and vanilla, beating until well blended. Gradually beat in the flour mixture. The dough will be stiff.

3. Divide the dough in half. With your hands, roll each half into a 12-inch log, then flatten slightly so each log is about 1¾ inches wide. Place the logs, 5 inches apart, on the prepared baking sheet and bake for 20 to 25 minutes, or until just firm. Transfer to a wire rack to cool for 10 minutes. Leave the oven on.

4. Transfer the logs to a work surface. With a serrated knife, slice the logs on the diagonal into scant ½-inch-thick slices. Place the slices on 2 ungreased baking sheets and bake, turning once, for 10 minutes, or until crisp. Transfer to a wire rack to cool before serving.

VALUES ARE PER COOKIE
FAT: 1G/18%
CALORIES: 51
SATURATED FAT: 0.4G
CARBOHYDRATE: 9G
PROTEIN: 1G
CHOLESTEROL: 6MG
SODIUM: 32MG

BERRY CAKE

SERVES: 8
WORKING TIME: 15 MINUTES
TOTAL TIME: 50 MINUTES PLUS COOLING TIME

1½ cups assorted whole berries (such as blackberries, blueberries, and raspberries)

1 cup flour

¾ cup plus 1 tablespoon granulated sugar

½ teaspoon baking soda

½ teaspoon ground ginger

¼ teaspoon salt

½ cup low-fat (1.5%) buttermilk

2 tablespoons vegetable oil

2 large eggs, lightly beaten

1. Preheat the oven to 375°. Spray an 8-inch round cake pan with nonstick cooking spray. In a small bowl, combine the berries; set aside.

2. In a medium bowl, combine the flour, ¾ cup of the sugar, the baking soda, ginger, and salt. Make a well in the center and pour in the buttermilk, oil, and eggs. Stir until no dry flour is visible.

3. Scrape the batter into the prepared pan. Spoon the berries on top and sprinkle with the remaining 1 tablespoon sugar. Bake for 35 to 40 minutes, or until a toothpick inserted in the center comes out clean. Cool in the pan on a wire rack. Remove from the pan, transfer to a plate, and serve.

Helpful hints: You can use any small berries for this recipe, except strawberries, which will add too much moisture. It's important to stir the dry ingredients thoroughly to mix them, and, conversely, to go easy on the mixing once you've added the liquid ingredients so that the cake turns out nice and tender.

This irresistible buttermilk cake is a snap to make, and it comes with its own garnish to boot; fresh berries peeking out from a crispy, glossy top. It's perfect for a convivial morning coffee klatch, a gracious afternoon tea, or a casual dinner with friends. Try it in the summer, when berries are cheap and plentiful.

FAT: 5G/22%
CALORIES: 207
SATURATED FAT: 1G
CARBOHYDRATE: 37G
PROTEIN: 4G
CHOLESTEROL: 54MG
SODIUM: 171MG

SINFREE CHOCOLATE INDULGENCE

SERVES: 10
WORKING TIME: 25 MINUTES
TOTAL TIME: 1 HOUR 15 MINUTES PLUS COOLING TIME

*A*lmost too good to be true, this dream dessert tastes like the moistest brownie imaginable, topped with a drizzle of tropical fruit purée.

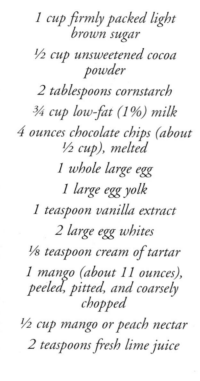

1 cup firmly packed light brown sugar

½ cup unsweetened cocoa powder

2 tablespoons cornstarch

¾ cup low-fat (1%) milk

4 ounces chocolate chips (about ½ cup), melted

1 whole large egg

1 large egg yolk

1 teaspoon vanilla extract

2 large egg whites

⅛ teaspoon cream of tartar

1 mango (about 11 ounces), peeled, pitted, and coarsely chopped

½ cup mango or peach nectar

2 teaspoons fresh lime juice

1. Preheat the oven to 350°. Spray an 8-inch round cake pan with nonstick cooking spray. Line the bottom of the pan with waxed paper.

2. In a medium bowl, combine the brown sugar, cocoa powder, and cornstarch. With an electric mixer, gradually beat in the milk and melted chocolate. Beat in the whole egg, egg yolk, and vanilla until the mixture is smooth. In a separate mixing bowl, with clean beaters, beat the egg whites and cream of tartar until stiff peaks form. Stir one-fourth of the egg whites into the batter to lighten, then gently fold in the remaining egg whites. Scrape the batter into the prepared pan, smoothing the top. Bake for 50 minutes or until a toothpick inserted in the center comes out almost clean (the cake will still be fairly wet). Transfer to a wire rack to cool completely.

3. Meanwhile, in a food processor or blender, combine the mango, mango nectar, and lime juice and process until smooth. Refrigerate until serving time. Drizzle half the mango sauce onto individual dessert plates. Top each with a slice of cake. Drizzle the remaining mango sauce over the cake slices and serve.

Helpful hint: Folding the egg whites into the batter in two stages helps preserve the volume of the beaten whites.

FAT: 5G/23%
CALORIES: 200
SATURATED FAT: 2.6G
CARBOHYDRATE: 39G
PROTEIN: 4G
CHOLESTEROL: 43MG
SODIUM: 38MG

PIES & TARTS

2

The filling of an angel pie floats in a fluffy cloud of meringue. Since the outside is angelically light, it's only right that the inside be devilishly rich—or at least taste that way. We've filled an almond-flavored meringue shell with chocolate custard, swirled in some vanilla yogurt "cream," and topped it all with almonds and chocolate chips.

CHOCOLATE-ALMOND ANGEL PIE

SERVES: 8
WORKING TIME: 25 MINUTES
TOTAL TIME: 1 HOUR 50 MINUTES PLUS DRAINING AND CHILLING TIME

½ recipe Vanilla Yogurt Topping
(p. 11)

¼ cup plus 1 tablespoon sliced
almonds, toasted

1 cup confectioners' sugar, sifted

½ cup egg whites (about 4 large)

½ teaspoon cream of tartar

½ cup superfine sugar

¼ teaspoon almond extract

3¼ cups low-fat (2%) milk

¾ cup firmly packed light brown
sugar

¼ cup plus 1½ teaspoons
unsweetened cocoa powder

⅓ cup cornstarch

¼ teaspoon cinnamon

3 ounces mini chocolate chips
(about 6 tablespoons)

1. Prepare the vanilla yogurt topping; set aside. In a food processor or blender, combine ¼ cup of the almonds and 1 tablespoon of the confectioners' sugar and process until finely ground; set aside.

2. Preheat the oven to 225°. In a large bowl, with an electric mixer, beat the egg whites and cream of tartar until soft peaks form. Gradually beat in the superfine sugar, 1 tablespoon at a time, until the whites are stiff and shiny, about 8 minutes. Halfway through, beat in the almond extract. Fold the remaining confectioners' sugar and the almond-sugar mixture into the egg whites. Spread the meringue over the bottom and up the sides of a 9-inch glass or ceramic pie plate (see tip). Bake for 1½ hours, or until crisp. Cool on a wire rack.

3. Meanwhile, in a medium saucepan, combine 2¾ cups of the milk and ½ cup of the brown sugar and bring to a boil over medium heat, stirring. In a small bowl, combine the cocoa, cornstarch, cinnamon, the remaining ¼ cup brown sugar, and remaining ½ cup milk. Whisk the cocoa mixture into the boiling milk mixture and cook, whisking constantly, until the mixture comes to a boil and is thickened, about 5 minutes. Remove from the heat and stir in ¼ cup of the chocolate chips. Cool to room temperature. Spoon the mixture into the pie shell, smoothing the top. Top with the yogurt mixture and swirl with a knife. Refrigerate 1 hour, top with the remaining chocolate chips and almonds, and serve.

FAT: 7G/18%
CALORIES: 353
SATURATED FAT: 3..4G
CARBOHYDRATE: 69G
PROTEIN: 7G
CHOLESTEROL: 9MG
SODIUM: 94MG

TIP

Using a rubber spatula, spread the meringue over the bottom of the pie plate in a thick layer (in order to support the filling). Continue spreading the meringue up the sides of the pie plate, but in a slightly thinner layer.

RASPBERRY PIE

SERVES: 8
WORKING TIME: 40 MINUTES
TOTAL TIME: 2 HOURS PLUS CHILLING AND COOLING TIME

The combination of raspberries and chocolate has become a modern classic. Here's a light but spectacular interpretation: A crisp chocolate meringue shell surrounds raspberries at their very best—gorgeous whole berries in a lightly sweetened, orange-scented raspberry purée. And if that weren't enough, hidden under the filling is a secret layer of rich chocolate.

Vanilla Yogurt Topping (p. 11)
½ cup egg whites (about 4 large)
½ teaspoon cream of tartar
¾ cup superfine sugar
½ teaspoon vanilla extract
1 cup confectioners' sugar
2 tablespoons unsweetened cocoa powder
12-ounce package unsweetened frozen raspberries, thawed
2 tablespoons orange juice
4 teaspoons cornstarch mixed with 2 tablespoons water
3 cups fresh raspberries
2 ounces chocolate chips (about ¼ cup), melted and cooled

1. Make the vanilla yogurt topping, but only let it drain 1 to 2 hours, or until called for in step 4.

2. Preheat the oven to 225°. In a large bowl, with an electric mixer, beat the egg whites and cream of tartar until soft peaks form. Gradually beat in ½ cup of the superfine sugar, 1 tablespoon at a time, until the whites are stiff and shiny, about 8 minutes. Halfway through, beat in the vanilla. Fold in the confectioners' sugar and cocoa powder. Spoon the meringue into a 9-inch glass or ceramic pie plate and, using a spatula, spread it over the bottom and up the sides of the pie plate (see tip on p. 53). Bake for 1½ hours, or until crisp. Cool on a wire rack.

3. In a food processor, combine the thawed raspberries, orange juice, and the remaining ¼ cup superfine sugar and process to a smooth purée. To remove the seeds, push the purée through a fine-mesh sieve set over a medium saucepan. Bring to a boil over medium heat, stir in the cornstarch mixture, and cook, stirring constantly, until thickened, about 1 minute. Remove from the heat and stir in 2 cups of the fresh raspberries. Set aside to cool to room temperature.

4. Brush the bottom of the pie shell with the melted chocolate. Top with the raspberry mixture and spoon the yogurt topping in the center. Sprinkle the pie with the remaining 1 cup fresh raspberries and chill for 1 hour before serving.

FAT: 3G/11%
CALORIES: 253
SATURATED FAT: 1.5G
CARBOHYDRATE: 56G
PROTEIN: 4G
CHOLESTEROL: 2MG
SODIUM: 45MG

PEAR TART

SERVES: 8
WORKING TIME: 45 MINUTES
TOTAL TIME: 1 HOUR 25 MINUTES PLUS CHILLING AND COOLING TIME

Basic Pie Dough (p. 10)
2 cups dry white wine
¾ cup granulated sugar
½ teaspoon cinnamon
½ teaspoon ground ginger
⅛ teaspoon freshly ground black pepper
2 pounds firm-ripe pears (about 4), peeled, cored, and cut into eighths
¾ cup low-fat (2%) milk
1 whole large egg
1 large egg white

1. Using a 9-inch tart pan with a removable bottom instead of a pie plate, prepare the pie dough through step 3. Leave the oven on.

2. Meanwhile, in a large saucepan, combine the wine, ½ cup of the sugar, the cinnamon, ginger, and pepper. Bring to a boil over medium heat, reduce the heat to a simmer, and carefully slip in the pears. Cover and cook until the pears are tender but not falling apart (a knife should pierce the pears, but there should still be some resistance). With a slotted spoon, transfer the pears to a plate; reserve the poaching liquid.

3. Place the tart shell on a baking sheet. Arrange the pear slices in the tart pan in a circular pattern. In a small bowl, whisk together the milk, the remaining ¼ cup sugar, the whole egg, and egg white. Pour the custard over the pears and bake for 45 minutes, or until the crust is golden brown and the custard is set. Cool the tart on a wire rack.

4. Meanwhile, bring the poaching liquid to a boil over high heat. Cook, without stirring, until it is reduced to a thick syrup (about ¼ cup), 8 to 10 minutes. Brush the warm glaze over the cooled tart. Serve at room temperature or chilled.

Helpful hint: Pears for cooking should be fragrant (which indicates that they will taste sweet) and firm-ripe, but not soft, or they will turn to mush when cooked.

FAT: 9G/26%
CALORIES: 308
SATURATED FAT: 2.9G
CARBOHYDRATE: 53G
PROTEIN: 5G
CHOLESTEROL: 33MG
SODIUM: 130MG

Though apple pie is the classic ending to a casual family meal, a company dinner calls for an elegant dessert such as this pear tart. The pears are cooked in spiced white wine, then arranged in the tart shell and covered with a custard that turns golden as the tart bakes. A spoonful of vanilla frozen yogurt would make the perfect accompaniment.

The
holidays just don't seem
complete without
pumpkin pie. But most
traditional recipes are
quite high in fat. We've
lightened our version
by using a reduced-fat
crust, replacing the
cream with evaporated
skimmed milk, and
substituting egg whites
for two of the whole
eggs. A wreath of
crunchy almond
praline makes our
pumpkin pie a true
standout.

PUMPKIN PRALINE PIE

SERVES: 10
WORKING TIME: 55 MINUTES
TOTAL TIME: 1 HOUR 40 MINUTES PLUS CHILLING AND COOLING TIME

Basic Pie Dough (p. 10)

½ cup granulated sugar

⅓ cup slivered almonds

15-ounce can solid-pack pumpkin purée

¾ cup firmly packed light brown sugar

1¼ cups evaporated skimmed milk

1 whole large egg

2 large egg whites

2 tablespoons bourbon or rum

1½ teaspoons cinnamon

½ teaspoon ground ginger

¼ teaspoon nutmeg

¼ teaspoon salt

⅛ teaspoon ground cloves

1. Prepare the pie dough through step 1. Meanwhile, line a baking sheet with foil; set aside. In a heavy saucepan, combine the granulated sugar and ¼ cup of water. Cook over low heat, stirring, until the sugar is dissolved. Increase the heat to high and cook, without stirring, until the sugar turns a medium amber, about 6 minutes. Immediately remove from the heat and add the almonds, stirring until well coated. Pour the almond mixture onto the baking sheet and with a metal spatula, quickly spread into a thin layer (see tip, top photo). Let the almond praline cool completely before touching.

2. Preheat the oven to 375°. On a lightly floured surface, roll the dough out to a 13-inch circle. Place the dough in a 9-inch glass or ceramic pie plate, forming a high fluted edge.

3. In a large bowl, with an electric mixer, combine the pumpkin, brown sugar, evaporated milk, whole egg, egg whites, bourbon, cinnamon, ginger, nutmeg, salt, and cloves, beating until well combined. Set the pie shell on a baking sheet on the oven rack. Pour the pumpkin filling into the pie shell and bake for 50 to 60 minutes, or until a knife inserted 1 inch from the edge comes out clean. Transfer to a wire rack to cool. Remove the praline from the foil and break into pieces (see tip, bottom photo). Sprinkle the pieces over the pie, or in a band around the outside, and serve at room temperature or slightly chilled.

FAT: 9G/27%
CALORIES: 296
SATURATED FAT: 2.4G
CARBOHYDRATE: 48G
PROTEIN: 7G
CHOLESTEROL: 26MG
SODIUM: 198MG

TIP

Spread the praline mixture quickly but carefully (melted sugar is much hotter than boiling water). When the praline is cool and hard, peel it off the foil and, with your hands, break it into bite-sized pieces.

KEY LIME PIE

SERVES: 8
WORKING TIME: 25 MINUTES
TOTAL TIME: 1 HOUR 10 MINUTES PLUS CHILLING AND COOLING TIME

Key lime pie originated in the Florida Keys more than a century ago, coinciding with the introduction of sweetened condensed milk—which has 960 calories and 24 grams of fat per cup. For our version of the pie, we've come up with a combination of lower-fat dairy products that successfully duplicates the condensed milk's dense, velvety texture, without sacrificing any of the rich flavor.

Graham Cracker Cookie Crust (p. 10)
2 whole large eggs
1 large egg white
⅔ cup granulated sugar
2 tablespoons flour
2 teaspoons grated lime zest
½ cup low-fat (1%) cottage cheese
½ cup evaporated whole milk
½ cup evaporated skimmed milk
⅔ cup fresh lime juice
⅓ cup reduced-fat whipped topping

1. Prepare the crust through step 2. Reduce the oven temperature to 350°.

2. Meanwhile, in a large bowl with an electric mixer, beat the whole eggs, egg white, sugar, flour, and 1 teaspoon of the lime zest until light and fluffy, about 5 minutes.

3. In a food processor or blender, process the cottage cheese until very smooth and creamy, about 1 minute. Gradually beat the cottage cheese purée, evaporated milks, and lime juice into the egg mixture, beating until just combined. Pour into the pie shell and bake for 35 minutes, or until just set. Cool on a wire rack and refrigerate until chilled.

4. Using a pastry bag with a #5 star tip (or a sturdy plastic bag with a small hole cut from the very tip of one corner), pipe the whipped topping in 10 small dollops on the surface of the pie. Sprinkle the dollops with the remaining 1 teaspoon lime zest and serve.

Helpful hints: To get the most juice from limes and other citrus fruits, roll them firmly on the counter before juicing. It also helps to warm the fruits by immersing them in hot water for a few minutes, or by microwaving them for 30 seconds. If you like, you can substitute 1 cup of evaporated low-fat milk for the evaporated whole and evaporated skimmed milks.

FAT: 9G/26%
CALORIES: 318
SATURATED FAT: 2.7G
CARBOHYDRATE: 52G
PROTEIN: 9G
CHOLESTEROL: 60MG
SODIUM: 310MG

DOUBLE BLUEBERRY PIE

SERVES: 8
WORKING TIME: 25 MINUTES
TOTAL TIME: 45 MINUTES PLUS COOLING TIME

Cooked blueberries have quite a different flavor and texture from fresh berries, and it's a treat to encounter both in a single pie.

*Crunchy Gingersnap Cookie
Crust (p. 10)*
⅔ cup granulated sugar
3 tablespoons cornstarch
1 teaspoon grated lemon zest
½ teaspoon cinnamon
⅛ teaspoon ground allspice
*⅛ teaspoon freshly ground
black pepper*
3 cups frozen blueberries
2 tablespoons fresh lemon juice
3 cups fresh blueberries

1. Prepare the gingersnap crust through step 2.

2. Meanwhile, in a small bowl, combine the sugar, cornstarch, lemon zest, cinnamon, allspice, and pepper. In a medium saucepan, combine the frozen blueberries and ¼ cup of water. Bring to a boil over medium heat. Stir in the sugar mixture and lemon juice. Return to a boil and cook, stirring frequently, until thickened, about 5 minutes. Remove from the heat and set aside to cool to room temperature.

3. Stir 2 cups of the fresh blueberries into the cooked blueberries and spoon into the pie shell. Top the pie with the remaining 1 cup fresh blueberries, cut into 8 wedges, and serve.

Helpful hint: You can make this pie using all fresh berries if you like. The cooking times will remain the same.

FAT: 6G/19%
CALORIES: 290
SATURATED FAT: 0.8G
CARBOHYDRATE: 60G
PROTEIN: 3G
CHOLESTEROL: 0MG
SODIUM: 192MG

BUTTERSCOTCH PIE

SERVES: 8
WORKING TIME: 20 MINUTES
TOTAL TIME: 35 MINUTES PLUS DRAINING AND COOLING TIME

*Butterscotch Cookie Crust
(p. 10)*

Vanilla Yogurt Topping (p. 11)

1 large egg

¼ cup cornstarch

2 cups low-fat (1%) milk

*⅔ cup firmly packed dark
brown sugar*

¼ teaspoon salt

1 teaspoon vanilla extract

1 vanilla wafer, crumbled

1. Prepare the butterscotch crust through step 2 and make the yogurt topping.

2. Meanwhile, in a small bowl, whisk the egg into the cornstarch until well combined. Whisk in ½ cup of the milk. In a medium saucepan, combine the remaining 1½ cups milk, the brown sugar, and salt. Bring to a boil over medium heat. Whisk about ½ cup of the hot milk mixture into the egg mixture, then whisk the warmed egg mixture back into the saucepan. Simmer, whisking, until thickened, about 1 minute. Remove the custard from the heat and stir in the vanilla. Spoon the mixture into the pie shell, smoothing the top.

3. Serve the pie at room temperature or chilled. Just before serving, cut the pie into 8 wedges. Top each piece with a dollop of the yogurt topping and sprinkle with the crumbled vanilla wafer.

Helpful hint: Be sure to follow the directions carefully in step 2 regarding warming or "tempering" the egg mixture with some of the hot milk. If the eggs are not warmed first, they may curdle when added to the boiling liquid.

FAT: 7G/22%
CALORIES: 281
SATURATED FAT: 1.5G
CARBOHYDRATE: 52G
PROTEIN: 6G
CHOLESTEROL: 31MG
SODIUM: 245MG

This smooth butterscotch custard (made with low-fat milk) will satisfy even the most discerning palates.

LEMON MERINGUE PIE

SERVES: 8
WORKING TIME: 30 MINUTES
TOTAL TIME: 1 HOUR 10 MINUTES PLUS CHILLING AND COOLING TIME

*L*emon meringue is definitely one of America's favorite pies. Its attraction lies in the delightful contrast between the flaky crust, the tart, smooth citrus filling, and the airy, sweet meringue. For our deceptively low-fat version we've simply used a low-fat crust and reduced the amount of butter and eggs in the filling. The meringue is already fat free.

Basic Pie Dough (p. 10)
1⅓ cups granulated sugar
⅓ cup cornstarch
¼ teaspoon salt
Two 3 x ½-inch strips of lemon zest
2 whole large eggs, lightly beaten
½ cup plus 1 teaspoon fresh lemon juice
2 teaspoons unsalted butter
3 large egg whites

1. Prepare the pie dough through step 3. Increase the oven temperature to 400°.

2. Meanwhile, in a medium saucepan, combine 1 cup of the sugar, the cornstarch, salt, and lemon zest. Add 1¾ cups of water, stirring until smooth. Bring to a boil over medium heat, reduce to a simmer, and cook, stirring occasionally, until thickened, about 5 minutes. Remove from the heat. Remove the lemon zest.

3. In a medium bowl, combine the eggs, ½ cup of the lemon juice, and the butter. Stirring constantly, gradually add the sugar mixture. Strain the mixture through a sieve into the pie shell. Bake for 10 minutes, or until the filling is just beginning to set.

4. Meanwhile, in another medium bowl, with an electric mixer, beat the egg whites and remaining 1 teaspoon lemon juice until soft peaks form. Gradually beat in the remaining ⅓ cup sugar until the whites are stiff and shiny. Pile the meringue lightly onto the pie, spreading it to the edge. Reduce the oven temperature to 325° and bake the pie for 20 minutes, or until the meringue is lightly browned and set. Refrigerate until chilled.

Helpful hint: Be sure to spread the meringue all the way to the edge of the filling so that it touches the crust all around. Otherwise, the meringue may shrink away from the edge while baking.

FAT: 10G/27%
CALORIES: 333
SATURATED FAT: 3.4G
CARBOHYDRATE: 56G
PROTEIN: 6G
CHOLESTEROL: 60MG
SODIUM: 205MG

CARAMEL TART WITH PECANS

SERVES: 10
WORKING TIME: 35 MINUTES
TOTAL TIME: 55 MINUTES PLUS CHILLING AND COOLING TIME

Basic Pie Dough (p. 10)

1 cup plus 2 tablespoons granulated sugar

1¾ cups low-fat (1%) milk

¼ teaspoon salt

2 tablespoons flour

2 large egg whites

1½ tablespoons bourbon or dark rum

1 teaspoon vanilla extract

3 tablespoons finely chopped pecans

1 tablespoon confectioners' sugar

1. Preheat the oven to 375°. Using a 9-inch tart pan with a removable bottom instead of a pie plate, prepare the pie dough through step 3. Meanwhile, in a medium saucepan, combine ¾ cup plus 2 tablespoons of the granulated sugar and ¼ cup of water. Cook over medium heat, stirring, until the sugar is dissolved. Cook, without stirring, until the mixture turns a medium amber, about 5 minutes. Remove from the heat and gradually stir in the milk (the sugar mixture will sputter and the sugar will bind). Return to the heat and cook, stirring, until the sugar has remelted, about 5 minutes. Stir in the salt.

2. In a small bowl, whisk together the flour and the remaining ¼ cup granulated sugar. Whisk in 1 cup of the milk mixture in driblets, then whisk the mixture back into the milk mixture in the pan. Bring to a boil and cook, whisking constantly, until the mixture is thickened, about 3 minutes. Remove from the heat. In a bowl, whisk 1 cup of the caramel into the egg whites, then lightly beat the egg whites into the saucepan. Stir in the bourbon and vanilla.

3. Place the tart shell on a baking sheet, sprinkle the pecans into the bottom, and pour the caramel mixture over. Bake for 25 to 30 minutes, or until the filling is just set but still slightly wobbly in the center. Cool on a wire rack, then remove the sides of the tart pan and sprinkle with confectioners' sugar. Cut into 10 wedges and serve.

FAT: 8G/29%
CALORIES: 249
SATURATED FAT: 2.3G
CARBOHYDRATE: 40G
PROTEIN: 4G
CHOLESTEROL: 5MG
SODIUM: 167MG

Pecan pie, our inspiration for this recipe, is often served in small portions, simply because it can be devastatingly rich and overwhelmingly sweet. Our tart has a more pleasing proportion of filling to crust, and we've lightened up the filling by leaving out the corn syrup, butter, and egg yolks. Because the pecans are chopped, you seem to get more per mouthful than if they were whole.

Banana Cream Pie

SERVES: 10
WORKING TIME: 15 MINUTES
TOTAL TIME: 35 MINUTES PLUS COOLING TIME

There's nothing like a banana cream pie to bring out the child in any pie-lover. Banana cream offers a gentle, innocent sweetness and a comforting, slightly gooey texture that no sophisticated "gourmet" dessert can match. We've reserved some of the bananas for the topping, so the pie is pretty as is—without the usual calorie-laden whipped-cream topping.

Gingersnap Cookie Crust (p. 10)
¼ cup cornstarch
1 large egg
2½ cups low-fat (1%) milk
½ cup granulated sugar
1 vanilla bean, split lengthwise, or 1 teaspoon vanilla extract
Two 2 x ½-inch strips of orange zest
¼ teaspoon nutmeg
⅛ teaspoon salt
1½ pounds bananas
2 tablespoons orange juice
3 tablespoons apricot jam

1. Prepare the crust through step 2.

2. Meanwhile, in a small bowl, whisk the cornstarch into the egg until well combined. Whisk in ½ cup of the milk. In a medium saucepan, combine the remaining 2 cups milk, the sugar, vanilla bean (if using), orange zest, nutmeg, and salt. Bring to a boil over medium heat. Whisk some of the hot milk mixture into the egg mixture, then whisk the warmed egg mixture back into the saucepan. Simmer, whisking, until thickened, about 1 minute. Remove the custard from the heat and stir in the vanilla extract (if using). Set aside to cool to room temperature. Remove the orange zest and the vanilla bean, if using.

3. Thinly slice the bananas and toss them with the orange juice to keep them from discoloring. Fold all but 1 cup of the bananas into the cooled custard. Spoon the filling into the pie shell, smoothing the top. Arrange the remaining 1 cup bananas in a decorative design on the top of the pie. In a small saucepan, melt the jam over medium heat. Strain the jam through a sieve, then brush the glaze over the banana slices on the top of the pie. Serve the pie at room temperature or chilled.

Helpful hint: The gingersnap crust offers a nicely spicy contrast to the mellow filling, but you could make the pie with a Graham Cracker or Chocolate-Graham Crust instead (recipes on p. 10).

FAT: 6G/19%
CALORIES: 278
SATURATED FAT: 1.4G
CARBOHYDRATE: 53G
PROTEIN: 5G
CHOLESTEROL: 24MG
SODIUM: 238MG

Shallow double-crust pies are thought to be an American invention: To the British, a pie more often consists of a deep basin of fruit bubbling with juices and covered with a single thick, flaky, golden crust. Fresh peaches touched with lemon are the perfect filling for a deep-dish pie. The accompanying lightly sweetened sour cream melts right into the warm fruit.

ENGLISH DEEP-DISH PEACH PIE

SERVES: 8
WORKING TIME: 25 MINUTES
TOTAL TIME: 55 MINUTES PLUS CHILLING AND COOLING TIME

Basic Pie Dough (p. 10)

3 pounds ripe peaches, peeled, pitted, and cut into ¼-inch-thick wedges

¾ cup plus 1 tablespoon granulated sugar

½ cup flour

2 tablespoons fresh lemon juice

⅓ cup reduced-fat sour cream

1. Prepare the pie dough through step 1.

2. Preheat the oven to 375°. In a large bowl, combine the peaches, ¾ cup of the sugar, the flour, and lemon juice. Toss to evenly coat the peaches. Transfer the peaches to a 9-inch deep-dish glass or ceramic pie plate.

3. On a lightly floured board, roll the dough out to a 13-inch circle. Drape the dough evenly over the peaches, trimming the dough to a ½-inch overhang; reserve the trimmings. Tuck the dough under at the rim of the pie plate to form a neat edge (see tip). With a small knife, make several neat slashes in the dough. If desired, roll out the reserved dough trimmings and, using a paring knife, cut out a small circle and 2 or 3 leaves and place them on top of the pie. Place the pie plate on a baking sheet and bake for 30 minutes, or until the crust is set and golden brown and the peaches are soft.

4. In a small bowl, stir together the sour cream and the remaining 1 tablespoon sugar. Serve the pie warm with the sweetened sour cream on the side.

Helpful hints: You can use this basic recipe to make an apple pie as well: Use 6 cups of peeled tart apple wedges in place of the peaches, reduce the flour to ¼ cup, and add 1 teaspoon of cinnamon along with the sugar in step 2. You may need to bake the pie about 10 minutes longer.

FAT: 9G/25%
CALORIES: 327
SATURATED FAT: 3.1G
CARBOHYDRATE: 58G
PROTEIN: 5G
CHOLESTEROL: 7MG
SODIUM: 106MG

TIP

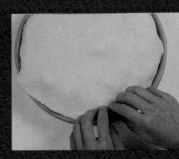

After placing the dough over the filling and trimming the excess, tuck the edge of the dough down between the pie plate and the peaches to form a smooth border.

COCONUT CREAM PIE

SERVES: 8
WORKING TIME: 15 MINUTES
TOTAL TIME: 1 HOUR 20 MINUTES PLUS COOLING TIME

Classic cream pies are made with whole milk, not cream; so substituting low-fat milk results in a more healthful dessert with no compromise in flavor. The coconut in this pie magically rises to the top of the filling as it bakes, ensuring that you get plenty of coconut flavor in every bite. To follow through with the tropical theme, garnish the pie with lime twists and slices of tropical fruit.

Toasted Oatmeal-Graham Cookie Crust (p. 10)
⅔ cup granulated sugar
¼ cup flour
1 whole large egg
2 large egg whites
2 cups low-fat (1%) milk
1 tablespoon dark rum
1 teaspoon coconut extract
½ teaspoon grated lime zest
½ cup flaked coconut

1. Prepare the crust through step 2 and set the pie shell aside to cool while you make the filling. Leave the oven on.

2. Meanwhile, in a medium bowl, combine the sugar and flour, whisking until well combined. Whisk in the whole egg, egg whites, milk, rum, coconut extract, lime zest, and flaked coconut. Pour the mixture into the cooled pie shell and bake until the custard is set, about 45 minutes. Set on a wire rack to cool.

3. Cut the pie into 8 wedges and serve at room temperature or chilled.

Helpful hint: For a more intense coconut flavor, toast the coconut before adding it to the custard: Spread the coconut in a shallow baking pan and toast it in a 325° oven, stirring occasionally, for about 10 minutes, or until the coconut is a light golden brown.

FAT: 8G/25%
CALORIES: 285
SATURATED FAT: 2.8G
CARBOHYDRATE: 48G
PROTEIN: 7G
CHOLESTEROL: 29MG
SODIUM: 195MG

CHOCOLATE VELVET TART

Serves: 8
Working time: 35 minutes
Total time: 1 hour 5 minutes plus cooling and chilling time

Serve this chocolaty tart on a special occasion, and be prepared to share the recipe: Of all the rich chocolate desserts around, this is one of the few that you can consume without guilt after a festive dinner. Vary the decorations as you wish: Instead of strips of paper, place a doily or cutouts (hearts, stars, or whatever you fancy) on the cake before dusting with sugar.

1¼ cups cake flour
½ cup granulated sugar
5 tablespoons unsweetened cocoa powder
½ teaspoon cinnamon
¼ teaspoon salt
2 large egg whites
¾ cup evaporated milk
1 tablespoon vegetable oil
2 whole large eggs
1 cup firmly packed light brown sugar
2 tablespoons all-purpose flour
½ cup light corn syrup
1 tablespoon bourbon or dark rum
2 ounces chocolate chips (about ¼ cup), melted
2 teaspoons confectioners' sugar

1. In a large bowl, combine the cake flour, granulated sugar, 2 tablespoons of the cocoa powder, the cinnamon, and salt. In a medium bowl, stir together the egg whites, ¼ cup of the evaporated milk, and the oil. Make a well in the center of the flour mixture and pour in the evaporated milk mixture, pulling in the flour mixture from the sides of the bowl until the dough just comes together. Wrap in plastic wrap and refrigerate 1 hour.

2. Preheat the oven to 350°. Spray a 9-inch tart pan with a removable bottom with nonstick cooking spray. Pat the dough into the prepared pan, coming up the sides to form a high edge.

3. In a medium bowl, whisk together the whole eggs, brown sugar, all-purpose flour, corn syrup, bourbon, melted chocolate, the remaining 3 tablespoons cocoa, and the remaining ½ cup evaporated milk. Pour into the prepared shell and bake for 30 minutes, or until the filling is puffed and just set. Cool on a wire rack for 30 minutes.

4. Using strips of paper, form a decorative pattern and dust the tart with the confectioners' sugar. Remove the paper strips and the sides of the tart pan and serve at room temperature or chilled.

Helpful hint: You can save time by making the dough the night before if you like. It will also be easier to handle after chilling overnight.

FAT: 7G/16%
CALORIES: 392
SATURATED FAT: 3.1G
CARBOHYDRATE: 80G
PROTEIN: 7G
CHOLESTEROL: 60MG
SODIUM: 159MG

CHERRY TARTLETS

SERVES: 8
WORKING TIME: 25 MINUTES
TOTAL TIME: 50 MINUTES PLUS CHILLING TIME

These enchanting little tarts (just 4 inches across) can be enjoyed at any time of year because they're made with jarred sour cherries.

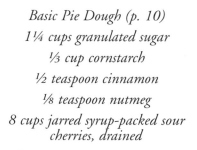

Basic Pie Dough (p. 10)
1¼ cups granulated sugar
⅓ cup cornstarch
½ teaspoon cinnamon
⅛ teaspoon nutmeg
8 cups jarred syrup-packed sour cherries, drained

1. Prepare the pie dough through step 1.

2. Preheat the oven to 375°. Spray eight 4-inch tartlet pans with removable bottoms with nonstick cooking spray. Divide the dough into 8 pieces. On a lightly floured surface, roll each piece of dough out to a 6-inch round. Fit the rounds into the prepared pans, pressing the dough into the bottom and sides of the pans. Place the pans on a large baking sheet.

3. In a large bowl, combine the sugar, cornstarch, cinnamon, and nutmeg. Add the cherries, tossing to coat. Spoon the cherry mixture into the prepared shells and bake for 25 minutes, or until the filling is piping hot and the crust is golden brown. Unmold the cherry tartlets and serve warm or chilled.

Helpful hints: Tartlet pans are sold in kitchenware shops and through mail-order cookware and baking supply catalogues. If you can't find any, you can make the tart in a 9-inch tart pan with a removable bottom. The baking time will remain the same.

FAT: 9G/15%
CALORIES: 525
SATURATED FAT: 2.5G
CARBOHYDRATE: 112G
PROTEIN: 4G
CHOLESTEROL: 4MG
SODIUM: 119MG

PUDDINGS & MOUSSES

3

BERRY TRIFLE

SERVES: 6
WORKING TIME: 25 MINUTES
TOTAL TIME: 30 MINUTES PLUS CHILLING TIME

Trifle is England's most distinguished dessert. Often served as the finale of afternoon tea, it's a layered creation of bite-sized pieces of cake and fruit, smothered in custard and whipped cream; sometimes trifle is saturated with sherry or Madeira. Our two-berry trifle is made with angel food (or nonfat loaf cake), slimmed-down custard sauce, and a light yogurt topping.

Vanilla Yogurt Topping (p. 11)

Vanilla Custard Sauce (p. 11)

2 cups unsweetened frozen strawberries, thawed

2 cups unsweetened frozen raspberries, thawed

¼ cup plus 2 tablespoons granulated sugar

¾ pound angel food cake or nonfat loaf cake, cut into 1-inch cubes

¼ cup fresh raspberries

1 tablespoon sliced almonds, toasted

1. Make the yogurt topping, but only let it drain 1 to 2 hours, or until called for in step 3. Make the custard sauce.

2. In a food processor, process the strawberries, raspberries, and sugar to a smooth purée. Push the mixture through a fine-mesh sieve set over a medium bowl to remove the seeds.

3. Spoon one-third of the custard sauce into the bottom of a 5-cup glass bowl. Top with one-third of the cake cubes, then one-third of the berry purée. Repeat the layering two more times using the same order of ingredients: custard sauce, cake, berry purée. Chill for 1 hour. Top with the yogurt topping and fresh raspberries, sprinkle with the almonds, and serve.

Helpful hint: Trifle is traditionally made in a glass bowl so that the colorful layers are visible. You can use another kind of bowl, if you like.

FAT: 3G/8%
CALORIES: 347
SATURATED FAT: 0.9G
CARBOHYDRATE: 74G
PROTEIN: 9G
CHOLESTEROL: 39MG
SODIUM: 482MG

PEANUT BUTTER CUP MOUSSE

SERVES: 4
WORKING TIME: 25 MINUTES
TOTAL TIME: 35 MINUTES PLUS CHILLING TIME

Heavy cream is featured in many mousse recipes, but this lush peanut-chocolate dessert is made with beaten evaporated skimmed milk and reduced-fat sour cream instead; gelatin is added to stabilize the mixture.

To decorate the mousse, spoon the melted chocolate into a small plastic bag, cut a small hole from the very tip of one corner, and squeeze the chocolate through it.

1½ cups low-fat (1%) milk

½ cup firmly packed dark brown sugar

4 teaspoons creamy peanut butter

¼ teaspoon salt

3 tablespoons cornstarch

1 large egg

2 tablespoons crème de cacao

½ teaspoon unflavored gelatin

½ cup evaporated skimmed milk

3 tablespoons reduced-fat sour cream

2 tablespoons granulated sugar

1 ounce chocolate chips (about 2 tablespoons), melted

2 teaspoons chopped peanuts

1. In a medium saucepan, combine 1 cup of the low-fat milk, ¼ cup of the brown sugar, the peanut butter, and salt. Bring to a boil over medium heat. In a small bowl, combine the cornstarch, the remaining ½ cup low-fat milk, and the remaining ¼ cup brown sugar. Whisk the cornstarch mixture into the milk mixture and cook, whisking, until thickened, about 5 minutes.

2. In a small bowl, lightly beat the egg. Gradually whisk some of the hot milk mixture into the egg, then whisk the warmed egg mixture back into the saucepan and bring to a boil over medium heat. Reduce the heat to low and cook, whisking constantly, until the mixture is thickened, about 2 minutes. Remove from the heat and stir in the crème de cacao. Cool to room temperature. Meanwhile, place ¼ cup of cold water in a small bowl, sprinkle the gelatin over, and let stand until softened, about 4 minutes. Set the bowl over a small saucepan of simmering water and stir until the gelatin dissolves, about 3 minutes. Set aside to cool to room temperature.

3. In a large bowl, with an electric mixer, beat the evaporated milk and sour cream until foamy. Gradually add the granulated sugar and beat until thickened. Beat in the dissolved gelatin until well combined. Fold the evaporated milk mixture into the peanut butter mixture, spoon into 4 bowls, and chill until set, about 2 hours. Drizzle the chocolate over the mousse, top with the peanuts, and serve.

FAT: 9G/23%
CALORIES: 347
SATURATED FAT: 3.5G
CARBOHYDRATE: 55G
PROTEIN: 10G
CHOLESTEROL: 62MG
SODIUM: 277MG

Individual Caramelized Citrus Puddings

Serves: 6
Working time: 15 minutes
Total time: 25 minutes plus chilling time

4 cups low-fat (1%) milk

1 cup granulated sugar

1 vanilla bean, split lengthwise, or 1 teaspoon vanilla extract

Three 3 x ½-inch strips of orange zest

Two 2 x ½-inch strips of lemon zest

Two 2 x ½-inch strips of lime zest

2 envelopes unflavored gelatin

¼ teaspoon nutmeg

1. In a medium saucepan, combine 3½ cups of the milk, ½ cup of the sugar, the vanilla bean (if using), the orange zest, lemon zest, and lime zest. Bring to a boil, remove from the heat, cover, and let steep for 20 minutes.

2. Meanwhile, in a small saucepan, combine the remaining ½ cup sugar and ¼ cup of water. Cook over medium heat, stirring, until the sugar is dissolved. Cook, without stirring, until the sugar is a medium amber color, about 4 minutes. Dividing evenly, pour the caramelized sugar into the bottoms of six 6-ounce custard cups or ramekins. Set aside. Place the remaining ½ cup milk in a small bowl and sprinkle the gelatin over. Let stand until softened, about 4 minutes.

3. Strain the milk-sugar mixture; discard the zests and save the vanilla bean for further use. Return the mixture to the saucepan, bring to a simmer, add the softened gelatin, and stir until dissolved. Remove from the heat and add the vanilla extract (if using). Pour the pudding into the prepared cups. Refrigerate until set, about 2 hours. Lightly dust each pudding with the nutmeg. To remove the puddings, run a knife around the edges of the cups, place a plate over each of the cups, and turn the cups over.

Helpful hint: You could also make this in eight 4-ounce cups if you'd like additional (but smaller) portions.

Fat: 2g/9%
Calories: 209
Saturated Fat: 1.1g
Carbohydrate: 42g
Protein: 7g
Cholesterol: 7mg
Sodium: 86mg

French restaurants will probably never cease to serve the perennial favorite, crème caramel. Also called crème renversée, it's a silky custard baked in a caramel-lined cup and then turned out so that the caramel sauce pools around the custard. Our version here—an unbaked variation from which we've eliminated the traditional cream and eggs—is a rich-tasting delight.

Triple Chocolate Pudding

Serves: 4
Working time: 15 minutes
Total time: 15 minutes plus chilling time

You can dive right into this intensely chocolaty pudding without a moment's hesitation: Even with its alluring topknot of whipped cream and chocolate shavings, it's still a low-fat treat. Like packaged pudding mixes, this recipe is based on cornstarch, but the resemblance ends there. No store-bought mix could ever be this deeply flavorful.

3 tablespoons unsweetened cocoa powder

3 tablespoons cornstarch

⅔ cup firmly packed dark brown sugar

3 cups low-fat (1%) milk

¼ teaspoon salt

1 vanilla bean, split lengthwise, or 1 teaspoon vanilla extract

2 ounces German sweet chocolate

1 ounce chocolate chips (about 2 tablespoons)

3 tablespoons whipped cream

2 teaspoons shaved chocolate (optional)

1. In a small bowl, combine the cocoa powder, cornstarch, ⅓ cup of the brown sugar, and ½ cup of the milk.

2. In a medium saucepan, combine the remaining 2½ cups milk, the remaining ⅓ cup brown sugar, the salt, and vanilla bean (if using). Bring to a boil over medium heat. Whisk the cocoa mixture into the boiling milk mixture and cook, whisking, just until thickened, about 4 minutes.

3. Stir in the sweet chocolate and chocolate chips, remove from the heat, and stir just until the chocolate is melted. Stir in the vanilla extract (if using). Spoon into 4 bowls and chill. Top with a dollop of whipped cream, sprinkle the shaved chocolate over, and serve.

Helpful hint: To make the chocolate shavings, have a bar of chocolate at room temperature and use a vegetable peeler to pare off thin shavings, letting them fall onto a plate. Pick up the shavings on the blade of a knife or with a metal spatula; they'll begin to melt if you handle them.

Fat: 12g/28%
Calories: 382
Saturated Fat: 6.9g
Carbohydrate: 67g
Protein: 8g
Cholesterol: 14mg
Sodium: 248mg

TANGERINE MOUSSE

SERVES: 4
WORKING TIME: 25 MINUTES
TOTAL TIME: 25 MINUTES PLUS COOLING AND CHILLING TIME

The contrast between tangy-sweet citrus flavor and velvety texture makes this a particularly pleasing dessert. For a low-fat mousse, heavy cream (just ¼ cup) is blended with reduced-fat sour cream before whipping. Buy large tangerines so the juicing goes quickly, and don't forget to grate the zest before you squeeze the fruit. You can even grate some extra zest and freeze it for future use.

1¼ teaspoons grated tangerine or orange zest

1¼ cups tangerine or orange juice

½ cup plus 3 tablespoons granulated sugar

⅛ teaspoon salt

3 tablespoons cornstarch

1 large egg

1 tablespoon fresh lemon juice

1 teaspoon unflavored gelatin

¼ cup heavy cream

¼ cup reduced-fat sour cream

2 tangerines, peeled and sectioned, or ½ cup canned mandarin orange segments, drained

1. In a medium saucepan, combine the tangerine zest, ¾ cup of the tangerine juice, ¼ cup of the sugar, and the salt. Bring to a boil over medium heat. In a small bowl, combine ¼ cup of the sugar, the cornstarch, and ¼ cup of the tangerine juice. Whisk the cornstarch mixture into the tangerine mixture and cook, whisking, until the mixture comes back to a boil and thickens, about 3 minutes.

2. In a small bowl, lightly beat the egg. Gradually whisk some of the hot tangerine mixture into the egg, then whisk the warmed egg mixture back into the saucepan and cook, whisking, until the mixture just comes to a boil, about 2 minutes. Remove from the heat and scrape into a medium bowl. Stir in the lemon juice and the remaining ¼ cup tangerine juice. Let cool to room temperature.

3. Meanwhile, place ¼ cup of cold water in a small bowl, sprinkle the gelatin over, and let stand until softened, about 4 minutes. Set the bowl over a small saucepan of simmering water and stir until the gelatin dissolves, about 3 minutes. Cool to room temperature.

4. In a large bowl, with an electric mixer, beat the cream and sour cream until foamy. Gradually beat in the remaining 3 tablespoons sugar and beat until soft peaks form. Beat in the dissolved gelatin until well combined. Fold the cream mixture into the tangerine mixture, spoon into 4 bowls, and chill until set, about 2 hours. Top with the tangerine sections and serve.

FAT: 9G/27%
CALORIES: 306
SATURATED FAT: 4.8G
CARBOHYDRATE: 54G
PROTEIN: 4G
CHOLESTEROL: 79MG
SODIUM: 102MG

Apple Bread Pudding

SERVES: 6
WORKING TIME: 20 MINUTES
TOTAL TIME: 45 MINUTES

*A*pples are simmered in cider here to intensify their flavor, and are then combined with bread and bathed in a vanilla egg custard.

1 pound Granny Smith apples, peeled, cored, and cut into ½-inch cubes

½ cup raisins

½ cup apple cider or juice

⅔ cup granulated sugar

2 cups low-fat (1%) milk

¼ cup evaporated low-fat milk

3 tablespoons reduced-fat sour cream

1 whole large egg

1 large egg white

1 teaspoon vanilla extract

¼ teaspoon salt

8 ounces white sandwich bread (about 8 slices), toasted and torn into large pieces

1. Preheat the oven to 350°. Spray an 8-cup glass or ceramic baking dish with nonstick cooking spray.

2. In a large nonstick skillet, combine the apples, raisins, and cider. Bring to a boil over medium heat, reduce to a simmer, cover, and cook until the apples are softened, about 5 minutes.

3. Meanwhile, in a large bowl, whisk together the sugar, low-fat milk, evaporated milk, sour cream, whole egg, egg white, vanilla, and salt. Place the toast pieces in the prepared baking dish along with the apple mixture. Pour the milk mixture on top and bake for 25 minutes, or until the custard is just set and the top is golden brown. Serve warm or at room temperature.

Helpful hints: If you like, Cortland or McIntosh apples can be used instead of the Granny Smiths. If you can't find evaporated low-fat milk, you can use evaporated skimmed milk instead.

FAT: 5G/13%
CALORIES: 345
SATURATED FAT: 1.6G
CARBOHYDRATE: 68G
PROTEIN: 9G
CHOLESTEROL: 43MG
SODIUM: 371MG

Butterscotch Pudding

SERVES: 4
WORKING TIME: 15 MINUTES
TOTAL TIME: 15 MINUTES PLUS CHILLING TIME

¼ cup cornstarch

⅔ cup firmly packed light brown sugar

3 cups low-fat (1%) milk

¼ teaspoon salt

1 large egg

1 tablespoon unsalted butter

1 teaspoon vanilla extract

3 tablespoons whipped cream

1. In a small bowl, whisk together the cornstarch, ⅓ cup of the brown sugar, and ½ cup of the milk. In a medium saucepan, combine the remaining 2½ cups milk, the remaining ⅓ cup brown sugar, and the salt. Bring to a boil over medium heat. Stir the cornstarch mixture into the boiling milk mixture and cook, stirring, until thickened, about 4 minutes.

2. In a small bowl, lightly beat the egg. Gradually whisk some of the hot milk mixture into the egg, then whisk the warmed egg mixture back into the saucepan. Return to the heat and cook, whisking constantly, for about 1 minute. Remove from the heat and stir in the butter and vanilla. Spoon into 4 dessert bowls and refrigerate until chilled, about 1 hour. With a #21 star tip and a pastry bag, pipe the whipped cream on top of the pudding (or, use a spoon to form small dollops) and serve.

Helpful hint: Mixing the cornstarch with a small amount of milk (in step 1) helps prevent the cornstarch from forming lumps when it's added to the hot milk.

FAT: 8G/23%
CALORIES: 310
SATURATED FAT: 4G
CARBOHYDRATE: 53G
PROTEIN: 8G
CHOLESTEROL: 74MG
SODIUM: 260MG

A *modest amount of butter is added at the last possible moment here so that its pure flavor shines through.*

MOCHA PUDDING CAKE

SERVES: 8
WORKING TIME: 25 MINUTES
TOTAL TIME: 55 MINUTES

If you find that the whole process of baking seems magical, this recipe will be even more astonishing than most. You mix the batter, sprinkle it with a mixture of cocoa powder and sugar, and pour hot water over it; forty minutes later you're swooning over a luscious, brownie-like chocolate cake with a thick, hot, fudgy sauce. Even more amazing: It's low in fat, too.

¾ cup firmly packed dark brown sugar

6 tablespoons plus 1½ teaspoons unsweetened cocoa powder

1 cup granulated sugar

2 tablespoons plus 1 teaspoon instant espresso powder

1 cup flour

2 teaspoons baking powder

¼ teaspoon cinnamon

¼ teaspoon salt

½ cup low-fat (1%) milk

¼ cup unsalted butter, melted

1 teaspoon vanilla extract

1¾ cups very hot water

1½ cups nonfat coffee frozen yogurt

1. Preheat the oven to 350°. In a small bowl, combine the brown sugar, ¼ cup of the cocoa powder, ¼ cup of the granulated sugar, and 1 teaspoon of the espresso powder. Set aside.

2. In a medium bowl, combine the flour, baking powder, cinnamon, salt, the remaining 2 tablespoons plus 1½ teaspoons cocoa powder, the remaining ¾ cup granulated sugar, and the remaining 2 tablespoons espresso powder. In a small bowl, combine the milk, butter, and vanilla. Stir the milk mixture into the flour mixture until well combined.

3. Scrape the batter into an ungreased 9-inch square baking pan. Sprinkle the reserved brown sugar mixture over the batter. Pour the hot water over and bake for 40 minutes, or until the top is set and the mixture is bubbly.

4. Divide the mocha pudding cake among 8 plates. Serve warm or at room temperature with a scoop of frozen yogurt alongside.

Helpful hint: You can substitute regular instant coffee if espresso powder is not available; use the powdered kind rather than freeze-dried crystals, which will not readily combine with the other dry ingredients.

FAT: 7G/19%
CALORIES: 341
SATURATED FAT: 4G
CARBOHYDRATE: 69G
PROTEIN: 4G
CHOLESTEROL: 16MG
SODIUM: 225MG

JASMINE RICE PUDDING

SERVES: 8
WORKING TIME: 10 MINUTES
TOTAL TIME: 40 MINUTES

*S*ave the raisins and cinnamon for another day: We've got more glorious things in store for our rice pudding, which is made with jasmine rice—a fragrant Thai rice with a hint of floral flavor. The rice is spiced with sweetly aromatic cardamom and studded with plump toasted pine nuts. An intensely flavorful apricot purée tops the pudding.

1 cup dried apricots
¾ cup plus 2 tablespoons granulated sugar
1½ cups jasmine rice
3 cups low-fat (1%) milk
½ teaspoon ground cardamom
¼ teaspoon salt
⅓ cup pine nuts

1. In a small saucepan, combine the apricots, 2 tablespoons of the sugar, and 1½ cups of water. Bring to a boil over medium heat, reduce to a simmer, cover, and cook until the apricots are very tender, about 30 minutes. Transfer the apricots and liquid to a food processor and process to a smooth purée.

2. Meanwhile, in a medium pot of boiling water, cook the rice for 10 minutes. Drain.

3. In a medium saucepan, combine the milk, the remaining ¾ cup sugar, the cardamom, and salt. Bring to a simmer over medium heat, add the drained rice, cover, and cook until the milk is reduced by half, about 15 minutes. Uncover and cook, stirring frequently, until the rice is very tender and creamy, about 10 minutes.

4. Meanwhile, in a small skillet, cook the pine nuts over medium heat until lightly toasted, about 2 minutes. Stir the pine nuts into the rice. Divide the pudding among 8 bowls and serve warm or at room temperature, topped with the apricot purée.

Helpful hint: Jasmine rice (available in Asian markets and many grocery stores) is similar in flavor to basmati rice, which is less expensive and can be used in this recipe. Texmati (even less expensive) or regular long-grain white rice can also be substituted for the jasmine if you like.

FAT: 4G/11%
CALORIES: 319
SATURATED FAT: 1.1G
CARBOHYDRATE: 65G
PROTEIN: 8G
CHOLESTEROL: 4MG
SODIUM: 117MG

LEMON MOUSSE WITH RASPBERRIES

SERVES: 4
WORKING TIME: 15 MINUTES
TOTAL TIME: 25 MINUTES PLUS CHILLING AND COOLING TIME

¾ cup plus 3 tablespoons
granulated sugar

3 tablespoons cornstarch

1 large egg, lightly beaten

1 teaspoon grated lemon zest

½ cup fresh lemon juice

⅛ teaspoon salt

½ teaspoon unflavored gelatin

⅓ cup heavy cream

3 tablespoons reduced-fat sour
cream, chilled

1 cup raspberries

1. In a medium saucepan, combine ¾ cup of the sugar and the cornstarch. Gradually whisk in 1 cup of cold water, stirring until smooth. Stir in the egg and cook over medium heat, whisking constantly, until the mixture comes to a boil, about 4 minutes. Remove from the heat and stir in the lemon zest, lemon juice, and salt. Set aside to cool to room temperature.

2. Meanwhile, place ¼ cup of cold water in a small bowl, sprinkle the gelatin over, and let stand until softened, about 4 minutes. Set the bowl over a small saucepan of simmering water and stir until the gelatin dissolves, about 3 minutes. Set aside to cool to room temperature.

3. In a medium bowl, with an electric mixer, beat the cream and the sour cream until foamy. Gradually beat in the remaining 3 tablespoons sugar until soft peaks form. Gradually beat in the dissolved gelatin.

4. Fold the cream mixture into the cooled lemon mixture. Spoon into 4 dessert glasses or bowls and chill until set, about 2 hours. Top with the raspberries and serve.

Helpful hint: Garnish each portion of berry-topped mousse with a curl of lemon zest. Be sure to peel the strips of zest before juicing the lemons.

FAT: 10G/27%
CALORIES: 333
SATURATED FAT: 5.7G
CARBOHYDRATE: 60G
PROTEIN: 3G
CHOLESTEROL: 84MG
SODIUM: 100MG

Delicate, delicious, highly perishable, and fairly pricey, raspberries are the royalty of domestic fruits. But just a handful of these blushing berries raises a simple dessert to elegant new heights. Here, they top a cool, creamy lemon mousse that's displayed to perfection in tall dessert glasses. Spherical "balloon" wineglasses or water goblets could also be used.

More than 100 years ago, Susan Stavers of Boston invented quick-cooking tapioca by grinding the starch of the South American manioc (cassava) root to create uniform granules. This dessert ingredient has been sold in packages since 1894. Tropical fruits are natural partners for tapioca; we've flavored the pudding with coconut extract, too.

Tropical Tapioca Pudding

Serves: 6
Working time: 15 minutes
Total time: 20 minutes

3 tablespoons fresh lime juice

3 tablespoons honey

1 mango, peeled and cut into ½-inch chunks (see tip)

1 banana, quartered lengthwise and cut into ½-inch-thick slices

1 cup raspberries

¼ cup quick-cooking tapioca

¼ cup granulated sugar

¼ teaspoon salt

2 cups low-fat (1%) milk

1 large egg

1½ teaspoons vanilla extract

½ teaspoon coconut extract

1. In a medium bowl, combine the lime juice and honey. Add the mango, banana, and raspberries, tossing to coat. Cover and refrigerate until serving time.

2. In a medium heavy-bottomed saucepan, combine the tapioca, sugar, and salt. Gradually stir in the milk. Bring to a boil, stirring constantly, and remove from the heat.

3. In a small bowl, lightly beat the egg. Gradually whisk some of the hot milk mixture into the egg, then whisk the warmed egg mixture back into the saucepan. Return to the heat and cook, stirring constantly, for 1 minute. Remove from the heat and stir in the vanilla and coconut extracts. Spoon into 6 dessert bowls and serve warm, at room temperature, or chilled, topped with the reserved fruit mixture.

Helpful hint: Tapioca thickens as it cools, so the pudding will be slightly stiffer if you serve it chilled.

Fat: 2g/9%
Calories: 191
Saturated Fat: 0.9g
Carbohydrate: 41g
Protein: 4g
Cholesterol: 39mg
Sodium: 173mg

TIP

Score each mango half into squares, cutting to, but not through, the skin. Turn the half inside out to pop the cut pieces outward. Cut the pieces away from the skin.

STRAWBERRY FOOL

SERVES: 4
WORKING TIME: 15 MINUTES
TOTAL TIME: 25 MINUTES PLUS CHILLING TIME

The word "fool" doesn't indicate that this dessert is lacking in intellect (although it is, indeed, simple). The name is thought to come from the French word "foulé," meaning crushed or puréed—that's how the berries in a fool are often prepared. We've made this old-fashioned English dessert more sensible by substituting low-fat yogurt for most of the whipped cream.

Vanilla Yogurt Topping (p. 11)
2½ pints strawberries
⅓ cup granulated sugar
¼ teaspoon cinnamon
¼ cup heavy cream

1. Make the yogurt topping, but only let it drain 1 to 2 hours, or until called for in step 4.

2. Slice enough strawberries to measure 1 cup and set aside. Halve the remaining strawberries.

3. In a medium saucepan, combine the halved strawberries, the sugar, cinnamon, and 2 tablespoons of water. Bring to a boil over high heat, reduce the heat to a simmer, and cook, stirring occasionally, until the fruit is softened, about 10 minutes. Transfer the strawberries and cooking liquid to a food processor or blender and process to a smooth purée. Scrape the purée into a medium bowl and refrigerate until chilled, about 1 hour.

4. Just before serving, in a small bowl, with an electric mixer, beat the cream until stiff peaks form. Fold the whipped cream into the drained yogurt. Fold the yogurt-cream mixture into the strawberry purée, leaving some swirls of white and red. Divide among 4 bowls, top with the sliced strawberries, and serve.

Helpful hint: Cream is easier to whip when it is well chilled. It also helps to have the bowl and beaters ice cold (you can place them in the freezer for 15 minutes before whipping the cream).

FAT: 7G/29%
CALORIES: 221
SATURATED FAT: 3.9G
CARBOHYDRATE: 38G
PROTEIN: 4G
CHOLESTEROL: 23MG
SODIUM: 45MG

Banana Pudding

SERVES: 4
WORKING TIME: 15 MINUTES
TOTAL TIME: 15 MINUTES PLUS COOLING AND CHILLING TIME

3 cups low-fat (1%) milk
⅔ cup granulated sugar
¼ teaspoon nutmeg
¼ teaspoon ground ginger
¼ teaspoon salt
¼ cup flour
1 large egg
1 teaspoon unsalted butter
¾ pound ripe bananas, cut into ½-inch slices
8 chocolate wafer cookies (2 ounces)

1. In a medium saucepan, combine the milk, ⅓ cup of the sugar, the nutmeg, ginger, and salt. Bring to a boil over medium heat. In a small bowl, whisk together the remaining ⅓ cup sugar and the flour. Stir into the milk mixture and cook, whisking, until thickened, about 1 minute.

2. In a small bowl, lightly beat the egg. Gradually whisk some of the hot milk mixture into the egg, then whisk the warmed egg mixture back into the saucepan. Return to the heat and cook, whisking, for 1 minute. Remove from the heat and stir in the butter. Set aside to cool to room temperature, then fold in all but 4 slices of the bananas.

3. Break the chocolate wafers into small pieces. Spoon half of the pudding into 4 bowls and top with a layer of cookies. Spoon in the remaining pudding. Chill at least 1 hour or as long as 8 hours. Before serving top each pudding with the remaining cookies and 1 of the reserved banana slices.

Helpful hint: To speed the ripening of green bananas, place them in a brown paper bag with half an apple and leave at room temperature.

Grown-up Southerners tend to be nostalgic about the "nanner" pudding they grew up with: vanilla pudding layered with sliced bananas and vanilla wafers. For our tempting update, the bananas are folded into a lightly spiced pudding and layered with crushed chocolate wafer cookies.

FAT: 7G/17%
CALORIES: 376
SATURATED FAT: 2.8G
CARBOHYDRATE: 72G
PROTEIN: 10G
CHOLESTEROL: 63MG
SODIUM: 326MG

STRAWBERRY CHEESECAKE MOUSSE

SERVES: 4
WORKING TIME: 20 MINUTES
TOTAL TIME: 20 MINUTES PLUS CHILLING TIME

Compare this recipe to one for a baked cheesecake and you'll notice that both the ingredient list and the preparation time have been dramatically shortened. Of course this isn't a cake— instead of baking the filling in a crust, we've spooned it into dessert bowls. The "cheesecake" mixture has a touch of tartness, and the flavor of the strawberries is underscored with a swirl of strawberry spreadable fruit.

½ teaspoon unflavored gelatin

2 pints fresh strawberries

2 tablespoons strawberry spreadable fruit

8 ounces nonfat cream cheese

¼ cup reduced-fat sour cream

½ cup granulated sugar

½ cup evaporated milk, chilled

1. Place ¼ cup of cold water in a small bowl, sprinkle the gelatin over, and let stand until softened, about 4 minutes. Set the bowl over a small saucepan of simmering water and stir until the gelatin dissolves, about 3 minutes. Set aside to cool.

2. Meanwhile, reserving 4 whole berries for a garnish, halve the strawberries. In a medium bowl, combine the halved fresh strawberries and the spreadable fruit, tossing until well coated.

3. In a food processor, combine the cream cheese, 2 tablespoons of the sour cream, and ¼ cup of the sugar and process until smooth. In a medium bowl, with an electric mixer, beat the evaporated milk with the remaining 2 tablespoons sour cream and remaining ¼ cup sugar until soft peaks form. Gradually beat in the cooled gelatin mixture.

4. Fold the cream cheese mixture into the evaporated milk mixture. Divide the strawberry mixture among 4 goblets or dessert bowls. Top with the "cheesecake" mixture and garnish with the reserved strawberries. Chill until set, about 1 hour, and serve.

Helpful hint: Spreadable fruit is like jam, but it is sweetened with fruit juice rather than sugar. It is used in this recipe because it is soft enough, even at room temperature, to coat the strawberries.

FAT: 5G/16%
CALORIES: 282
SATURATED FAT: 2.5G
CARBOHYDRATE: 49G
PROTEIN: 12G
CHOLESTEROL: 20MG
SODIUM: 314MG

MOCHACCINO BAVARIAN CREAM

SERVES: 4
WORKING TIME: 25 MINUTES
TOTAL TIME: 25 MINUTES PLUS CHILLING TIME

With elaborate coffee drinks becoming so popular, a chocolate mocha dessert—especially a low-fat one—is bound to be a hit.

Vanilla Yogurt Topping (p. 11)
1 cup low-fat (1%) milk
1 envelope unflavored gelatin
2 large eggs
½ cup granulated sugar
¼ cup unsweetened cocoa powder
1 tablespoon instant espresso powder
½ cup plain nonfat yogurt
3 tablespoons reduced-fat sour cream
12 chocolate-covered coffee beans (optional)

1. Make the yogurt topping.

2. Meanwhile, place ¼ cup of the milk in a small bowl, sprinkle the gelatin over, and let stand until softened, about 4 minutes.

3. In a medium bowl, combine the remaining ¾ cup milk, the eggs, sugar, cocoa, and espresso powder. Place the bowl over a saucepan of simmering water and cook, whisking, until the custard is slightly thickened, about 5 minutes. Add the softened gelatin and cook, whisking, until the gelatin is dissolved, about 2 minutes. Remove from the heat and let cool to room temperature.

4. Fold the plain yogurt and sour cream into the custard mixture. Spoon the mixture into 4 dessert bowls or glasses and refrigerate until chilled and set, about 2 hours. Top with a dollop of the yogurt topping, sprinkle with the coffee beans, and serve.

Helpful hint: Look for chocolate-covered coffee beans at candy stores and gourmet shops. You may even find a decaffeinated version.

FAT: 6G/21%
CALORIES: 262
SATURATED FAT: 2.8G
CARBOHYDRATE: 42G
PROTEIN: 13G
CHOLESTEROL: 116MG
SODIUM: 132MG

FROZEN DESSERTS

4

BISCUIT TORTONI

SERVES: 8
WORKING TIME: 15 MINUTES
TOTAL TIME: 25 MINUTES PLUS FREEZING TIME

In nineteenth-century Paris, Signore B. Tortoni ran an Italian restaurant and ice-cream parlor and one of his specialties was a rich frozen mousse topped with chopped almonds. Our version of this classic is made with evaporated skimmed milk in place of cream. We've flavored the dessert with almond liqueur and rum; you can use all rum or all liqueur, if you like.

½ cup plus 2 tablespoons granulated sugar
2 tablespoons cornstarch
2½ cups evaporated skimmed milk
⅛ teaspoon salt
1 large egg
2 tablespoons amaretto
1 tablespoon dark rum
1 teaspoon vanilla extract
¼ cup reduced-fat sour cream
2 ounces amaretti cookies, crumbled
1 tablespoon sliced almonds, toasted

1. In a small bowl, whisk together ¼ cup of the sugar, the cornstarch, and ½ cup of the evaporated milk. In a medium saucepan, combine 1½ cups of the evaporated milk, ¼ cup of the sugar, and the salt. Bring to a boil over medium heat. Whisk the cornstarch mixture into the milk mixture and cook, stirring constantly, until thickened, about 3 minutes. Remove from the heat.

2. In a small bowl, lightly beat the egg. Gradually whisk some of the hot milk mixture into the egg, then whisk the warmed egg mixture back into the saucepan. Return to the heat and cook, whisking constantly, for 1 minute. Remove from the heat and stir in the amaretto, rum, and vanilla. Cool the custard to room temperature.

3. In a small bowl, with an electric mixer, beat the remaining ½ cup evaporated milk and the sour cream until thick. Gradually beat in the remaining 2 tablespoons sugar until the mixture has doubled in volume. Fold the sour cream mixture into the custard. Line 8 cups of a muffin tin with paper liners. Divide the mixture evenly among the lined cups. Sprinkle the amaretti cookies and almonds over and freeze until set, about 3 hours.

Helpful hint: Amaretti are Italian macaroons made of sugar, egg whites, and apricot-kernel paste (which has a strong almond flavor). Look for them in the gourmet or imported foods aisle of your supermarket, at gourmet shops, and in Italian food stores.

FAT: 3G/13%
CALORIES: 203
SATURATED FAT: 0.8G
CARBOHYDRATE: 34G
PROTEIN: 8G
CHOLESTEROL: 32MG
SODIUM: 142MG

To capture the lovely flavor of hazelnuts in a low-fat mousse, we've flavored this mixture with Frangelico, a hazelnut-flavored liqueur, and we use just one ounce of nuts as a topping. Be careful, when chopping the nuts, not to run the machine too long, or you'll end up with hazelnut butter.

Frozen Hazelnut Mousse

SERVES: 4
WORKING TIME: 15 MINUTES
TOTAL TIME: 35 MINUTES PLUS FREEZING TIME

1 ounce hazelnuts
½ cup granulated sugar
3 tablespoons flour
2¼ cups low-fat (1%) milk
1 tablespoon light corn syrup
¼ teaspoon salt
1 large egg
2 tablespoons reduced-fat sour cream
3 tablespoons Frangelico
¼ teaspoon almond extract

1. Preheat the oven to 375°. Toast the hazelnuts until they are fragrant and the skins begin to pop, about 7 minutes (see tip, top photo). Rub the nuts in a cloth to remove the skin (bottom photo), then transfer to a food processor and pulse until coarsely chopped.

2. In a small bowl, stir together ¼ cup of the sugar and the flour. In a medium saucepan, combine the milk, the remaining ¼ cup sugar, the corn syrup, and salt. Bring to a boil over medium heat. Whisk the flour mixture into the milk mixture and cook, stirring constantly, until thickened, about 5 minutes.

3. In a small bowl, lightly beat the egg. Gradually whisk some of the hot milk mixture into the egg, then whisk the warmed egg mixture back into the saucepan. Return to the heat and cook, whisking constantly, for 2 minutes. Remove from the heat and cool to room temperature. Stir in the sour cream, Frangelico, and almond extract. Spoon into four 6- to 8-ounce goblets and freeze until solid. Let sit at room temperature for 20 minutes, top with the hazelnuts, and serve.

Helpful hint: Corn syrup prevents sugar from crystallizing, thereby assuring a silky texture in frozen desserts.

FAT: 8G/24%
CALORIES: 298
SATURATED FAT: 2.1G
CARBOHYDRATE: 45G
PROTEIN: 8G
CHOLESTEROL: 61MG
SODIUM: 230MG

TIP

To remove the inner skin from shelled hazelnuts, first spread the nuts in a shallow pan and toast them in a 375° oven. Turn the toasted nuts onto a kitchen towel and rub them in the towel; don't worry if flecks of the skin remain here and there on the nuts.

Caramel-Almond Ice Milk

Serves: 6
Working time: 20 minutes
Total time: 20 minutes plus chilling and freezing time

½ cup sliced almonds
1¼ cups granulated sugar
3 cups low-fat (1%) milk
1 tablespoon cornstarch mixed with 1 tablespoon water
1 ounce mini chocolate chips (about 2 tablespoons)

1. Preheat the oven to 350°. Place the almonds on a baking sheet and toast until golden brown and fragrant, about 5 minutes.

2. In a large saucepan, combine the sugar and ¼ cup of water. Bring to a boil over medium heat, stirring until the sugar is dissolved. Cook, without stirring, until the sugar is a medium amber color, about 5 minutes. Remove from the heat and gradually stir in the milk (the sugar syrup will sputter and the sugar will bind). Return to the heat and cook, stirring frequently, until the sugar has remelted, about 4 minutes. Bring the caramel to a boil, stir in the cornstarch mixture, and cook, stirring constantly, until slightly thickened, about 1 minute.

3. Refrigerate until well chilled, about 30 minutes, then transfer to the canister of an ice cream maker and freeze according to the manufacturer's directions. Shortly before the ice milk is frozen, add the almonds and chocolate chips and continue to freeze. Divide the ice milk among 6 bowls and serve.

Helpful hints: You'll need an ice cream maker (electric or hand cranked) for this recipe. If you often make frozen desserts at home, an electric model that doesn't require crushed ice will save you quite a bit of effort. Be careful when caramelizing the sugar: Melted sugar is considerably hotter than boiling water, and the sugar will sputter when you add the milk. To be safe, protect your hands with oven mitts or pot holders.

Fat: 7g/22%
Calories: 286
Saturated Fat: 2g
Carbohydrate: 53g
Protein: 6g
Cholesterol: 5mg
Sodium: 63mg

Some people think the best part of ice cream is the stuff that's "mixed in," whether it be crumbled cookies, bits of peppermint candy, or sliced strawberries. Those who agree will be delighted with this rich-tasting caramel ice milk, which is dotted with crisp toasted almonds and semisweet chocolate. It's hard to believe just five ingredients go into this fabulous dessert.

PEAR-RASPBERRY SHERBET

SERVES: 4
WORKING TIME: 25 MINUTES
TOTAL TIME: 25 MINUTES PLUS CHILLING AND FREEZING TIME

This Italian-style fruit-and-cream sherbet is meant to be eaten when it's still partially frozen—"semifreddo"—rather than rock hard. The raspberry flavor is reinforced with raspberry jam and liqueur. You can make the sherbet up to a day in advance: Cover the desserts and let them freeze solid, but allow them to soften at room temperature for 20 minutes before serving.

1 envelope unflavored gelatin

2 ripe pears, peeled, cored, and thinly sliced

½ cup pear nectar

1 tablespoon fresh lemon juice

⅔ cup low-fat (1.5%) buttermilk

½ cup granulated sugar

2 tablespoons reduced-fat cream cheese (Neufchâtel)

12-ounce package unsweetened frozen raspberries, thawed

¼ cup seedless raspberry jam

1 tablespoon raspberry liqueur

2 tablespoons whipped cream

⅓ cup fresh raspberries

1. Place ¼ cup of cold water in a small bowl, sprinkle the gelatin over, and let stand until softened, about 4 minutes. Set the bowl over a small saucepan of simmering water and stir until the gelatin dissolves, about 3 minutes. Cool to room temperature. In a small skillet, combine the pears, pear nectar, and lemon juice. Cook over medium heat, stirring occasionally, until softened, about 5 minutes. Transfer to a food processor and add ⅓ cup of the buttermilk, ¼ cup of the sugar, and the cream cheese. Process until smooth and transfer to a small bowl. Stir in half of the gelatin mixture. Cool to room temperature.

2. In the food processor, purée the frozen raspberries and the remaining ¼ cup sugar. Push the purée through a fine-mesh sieve to remove the seeds. Transfer to a small saucepan along with the remaining ⅓ cup buttermilk, the jam, and raspberry liqueur. Bring the purée to a gentle simmer over low heat. Stir in the remaining gelatin mixture and cook for 1 minute. Transfer to a small bowl and cool to room temperature.

3. Refrigerate the fruit mixtures, stirring occasionally, until slightly mounded, about 45 minutes. Spoon the mixtures in alternating layers into 4 parfait glasses. Freeze until almost, but not quite, frozen, about 1 hour. Top with the whipped cream and fresh raspberries and serve.

FAT: 4G/11%
CALORIES: 330
SATURATED FAT: 2G
CARBOHYDRATE: 72G
PROTEIN: 5G
CHOLESTEROL: 10MG
SODIUM: 73MG

MEXICAN CHOCOLATE ICE

SERVES: 4
WORKING TIME: 10 MINUTES
TOTAL TIME: 20 MINUTES PLUS FREEZING TIME

Dark,
sweet Mexican hot
chocolate, which is
spiced with cinnamon
and flavored with
vanilla and almonds,
inspired this dessert.

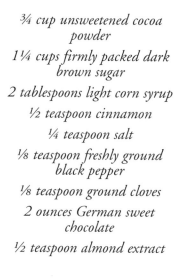

¾ cup unsweetened cocoa
powder

1¼ cups firmly packed dark
brown sugar

2 tablespoons light corn syrup

½ teaspoon cinnamon

¼ teaspoon salt

⅛ teaspoon freshly ground
black pepper

⅛ teaspoon ground cloves

2 ounces German sweet
chocolate

½ teaspoon almond extract

1. In a medium saucepan, combine the cocoa powder, brown sugar, corn syrup, cinnamon, salt, pepper, and cloves. Gradually whisk in 3 cups of water until smooth. Bring to a boil over medium heat and cook until well combined and slightly reduced, about 5 minutes. Add the sweet chocolate and stir until melted. Remove from the heat and cool to room temperature. Stir in the almond extract.

2. Pour the mixture into a 13 x 9-inch glass pan and freeze until frozen around the edges and beginning to solidify but still mushy in the center, about 2 hours. Stir, breaking up the ice crystals. Return to the freezer and freeze until solid, about 2 hours. Divide among 4 bowls and serve.

Helpful hint: German sweet chocolate is a dark, sweet cooking and baking chocolate sold in 4-ounce bars. You can substitute another dark, sweet chocolate if you like, but don't use milk chocolate or the flavor will not be as rich.

FAT: 7G/16%
CALORIES: 399
SATURATED FAT: 4.1G
CARBOHYDRATE: 92G
PROTEIN: 4G
CHOLESTEROL: 0MG
SODIUM: 180MG

Lemon-Buttermilk Sherbet

SERVES: 4
WORKING TIME: 15 MINUTES
TOTAL TIME: 15 MINUTES PLUS CHILLING AND FREEZING TIME

¾ cup granulated sugar

2 tablespoons cornstarch

2 teaspoons grated lemon zest

½ cup fresh lemon juice

3 tablespoons light corn syrup

3 cups low-fat (1.5%) buttermilk

2 tablespoons vodka or gin

1. In a medium saucepan, combine the sugar, cornstarch, and lemon zest. Add ¾ cup of water, stirring until smooth. Bring to a boil over medium heat, reduce to a simmer, and cook, stirring frequently, until thickened, about 10 minutes. Remove from the heat and stir in the lemon juice and corn syrup, whisking until well combined. Cool to room temperature.

2. Stir the buttermilk and vodka into the lemon mixture and refrigerate for 30 minutes. Transfer to the canister of an ice cream maker and freeze according to the manufacturer's directions. Divide among 4 bowls and serve.

Helpful hint: You can consider the alcohol optional; leave it out if you're serving the sherbet to children. Garnish each serving with a twisted lemon slice or a curl of lemon zest.

FAT: 3G/9%
CALORIES: 318
SATURATED FAT: 1.9G
CARBOHYDRATE: 65G
PROTEIN: 7G
CHOLESTEROL: 11MG
SODIUM: 113MG

L*ow-fat buttermilk makes this a smooth, tangy sherbet; vodka makes it breathtakingly sophisticated.*

ESPRESSO GRANITA

SERVES: 4
WORKING TIME: 10 MINUTES
TOTAL TIME: 20 MINUTES PLUS FREEZING TIME

*G*ranita *is a unique Italian ice with a crunchy, granular texture; coffee is the most popular flavor. In order to create the desired graininess, you need to break up the ice crystals by stirring the mixture as it begins to freeze. Granita is usually served with whipped cream; we've substituted a sweetened blend of nonfat yogurt and reduced-fat sour cream.*

4 cups freshly brewed coffee

1 tablespoon instant espresso powder

1 cup granulated sugar

1 vanilla bean, split lengthwise, or 1 teaspoon vanilla extract

Two 3 x ½-inch strips of lemon zest

⅓ cup plain nonfat yogurt

3 tablespoons reduced-fat sour cream

1. In a medium saucepan, combine the coffee, espresso powder, all but 2 tablespoons of the sugar, the vanilla bean (if using), and the lemon zest. Bring to a boil and cook for 5 minutes. Cool to room temperature. Discard the lemon zest and save the vanilla bean for furthur use. If using vanilla extract, stir it in after the mixture has cooled.

2. Pour the mixture into a 13 x 9-inch glass pan and freeze until frozen around the edges and beginning to get solid but still mushy in the center, about 2 hours. Stir, breaking up the ice crystals. Return to the freezer and freeze until just solid in the center and frozen around the edges, about 1 hour.

3. Meanwhile, in a small bowl, combine the yogurt, sour cream, and remaining 2 tablespoons sugar. Divide the granita among 4 bowls, top with the yogurt mixture, and serve.

Helpful hint: If you use a whole vanilla bean, rinse it, let it dry at room temperature, and then bury it in a container of sugar; use the vanilla-flavored sugar for baking.

FAT: 2G/8%
CALORIES: 233
SATURATED FAT: 0.8G
CARBOHYDRATE: 54G
PROTEIN: 2G
CHOLESTEROL: 4MG
SODIUM: 26MG

SPIKED STRAWBERRY-RASPBERRY SORBET

SERVES: 4
WORKING TIME: 10 MINUTES
TOTAL TIME: 10 MINUTES PLUS FREEZING TIME

*S*orbets capture the pure flavor of fruit in all its delicious intensity; this one has the added double punch of tequila and orange liqueur, making it a sort of frozen berry margarita. We've used frozen raspberries and strawberries, so you can serve this splendid dessert at any time of year. Garnish the sorbet with a few fresh berries, or top it with thin strips of orange and lime zest.

12-ounce package unsweetened frozen raspberries, thawed

12-ounce package unsweetened frozen strawberries, thawed

¾ cup granulated sugar

¼ cup fresh lime juice

3 tablespoons honey

2 tablespoons tequila or vodka

2 tablespoons orange liqueur (such as Triple Sec) or orange juice

1. In a food processor, combine the raspberries, strawberries, sugar, lime juice, honey, tequila, and orange liqueur and process to a smooth purée. Push the purée through a strainer to remove the seeds.

2. Transfer the fruit purée to the canister of an ice cream maker and freeze according to the manufacturer's directions. Divide among 4 bowls and serve.

Helpful hint: Use exactly the amounts of tequila and liqueur called for in the recipe: Alcohol lowers the freezing point of the mixture, and if you add too much alcohol, the sorbet may not freeze to the right consistency.

FAT: 1G/3%
CALORIES: 313
SATURATED FAT: 0G
CARBOHYDRATE: 74G
PROTEIN: 1G
CHOLESTEROL: 0MG
SODIUM: 3MG

When you want something more elegant than a simple scoop of rum-raisin, try this recipe. Traditionally, this Italian dessert would be made with mascarpone, a buttery Italian cheese. However, our velvety blend of cottage cheese, ricotta, and sour cream has far less fat and still produces a semifreddo that is sinfully delicious.

Honey Rum-Raisin Semifreddo

SERVES: 8
WORKING TIME: 15 MINUTES
TOTAL TIME: 15 MINUTES PLUS FREEZING TIME

½ cup raisins

¼ cup dark rum

2 cups low-fat (1%) cottage cheese

⅔ cup part-skim ricotta cheese

⅔ cup honey

¼ cup reduced-fat sour cream

⅛ teaspoon nutmeg

4 ounces chocolate chips (about ½ cup), melted

1. In a small bowl, stir together the raisins and rum. Set aside to soak for 10 minutes.

2. In a food processor, combine the cottage cheese, ricotta, honey, sour cream, and nutmeg and process until smooth, about 2 minutes. Transfer the mixture to a bowl and fold in the raisins and their soaking liquid.

3. Tear off eight 6-inch lengths of plastic wrap to line eight 2½-inch muffin-tin cups (see tip; top photo). Spoon the mixture into the prepared cups (bottom photo), cover with the plastic wrap, and freeze until firm, about 3 hours.

4. Drizzle the melted chocolate onto 8 dessert plates. Or, if desired, place the chocolate in a sturdy plastic bag, cut a small hole from the very tip of one corner and pipe the chocolate in a decorative pattern onto the plates. Unmold each semifreddo onto the chocolate and serve.

Helpful hint: To unmold a semifreddo, pull on the ends of the plastic wrap to lift it from the muffin-tin cup and invert the semifreddo onto a plate. Carefully peel away the plastic wrap. If necessary, place the finished portions in the freezer while you complete the remaining servings.

FAT: 7G/23%
CALORIES: 278
SATURATED FAT: 4.2G
CARBOHYDRATE: 43G
PROTEIN: 11G
CHOLESTEROL: 11MG
SODIUM: 262MG

TIP

Center a strip of plastic wrap in each of the muffin-tin cups, leaving overhang on each side. After dividing the cottage-cheese mixture evenly among the prepared cups, fold the ends of plastic wrap over the mixture.

PINEAPPLE-MANGO FROZEN YOGURT

SERVES: 4
WORKING TIME: 15 MINUTES
TOTAL TIME: 15 MINUTES PLUS FREEZING TIME

3 mangos, peeled, pitted, and sliced

1 cup fresh or juice-packed canned pineapple wedges, drained

⅓ cup granulated sugar

1 teaspoon grated lime zest

2 tablespoons fresh lime juice

2 tablespoons light corn syrup

1½ cups plain nonfat yogurt

¼ cup reduced-fat sour cream

¼ cup chopped fresh mint

1. Spread 2 of the mangos and the pineapple out on a baking sheet and place in the freezer until frozen solid. Slice the remaining mango; set aside.

2. In a food processor, combine the sugar, lime zest, lime juice, corn syrup, yogurt, sour cream, and mint and process until smooth. Add the frozen mango and pineapple and process until well blended but some chunks remain. Divide among 4 bowls, top with the reserved mango slices, and serve immediately.

Helpful hint: You can prepare this frozen yogurt ahead of time: After adding and processing the frozen fruit, pack the mixture into a container, cover, and refreeze it. Let the frozen yogurt soften at room temperature for 20 minutes before serving.

FAT: 3G/9%
CALORIES: 288
SATURATED FAT: 1.2G
CARBOHYDRATE: 64G
PROTEIN: 7G
CHOLESTEROL: 7MG
SODIUM: 89MG

A quick method of making frozen desserts is to cut fruit into chunks, freeze it, and then purée the fruit in a food processor. Here, mango and pineapple, two of the sweetest, most delectable tropical fruits, are combined with sweetened yogurt and the refreshing flavors of mint and lime. For an added touch, garnish each serving of yogurt with a fresh mint sprig.

BLUEBERRY BUTTERMILK SHERBET

SERVES: 4
WORKING TIME: 10 MINUTES
TOTAL TIME: 20 MINUTES PLUS FREEZING TIME

There's an old-fashioned New England feeling to this dessert, which features a homey combination of blueberries, buttermilk, and maple syrup. The buttermilk, though low in fat, yields a rich-tasting sherbet; maple syrup adds a special mellow sweetness. Ground ginger and allspice (like cinnamon, which is more commonly used with blueberries) point up the flavor of the berries.

¾ cup granulated sugar
2 tablespoons maple syrup
1 teaspoon grated lime zest
½ teaspoon ground ginger
⅛ teaspoon ground allspice
⅛ teaspoon salt
4 cups frozen blueberries
2 tablespoons cornstarch
2½ cups low-fat (1.5%) buttermilk
1 tablespoon fresh lime juice

1. In a medium saucepan, combine ½ cup of the sugar, the maple syrup, lime zest, ginger, allspice, and salt. Stir in the blueberries and cook over medium heat, stirring frequently, until the berries are tender and syrupy, about 7 minutes.

2. In a small bowl, combine the remaining ¼ cup sugar and the cornstarch. Stir the cornstarch mixture into the simmering blueberries and cook, stirring constantly, until thickened, about 2 minutes. Remove from the heat and cool to room temperature.

3. Stir in the buttermilk and lime juice. Transfer to the canister of an ice cream maker and freeze according to the manufacturer's directions.

Helpful hint: When they're in season, make this dessert with fresh blueberries instead of frozen.

FAT: 4G/11%
CALORIES: 343
SATURATED FAT: 1.6G
CARBOHYDRATE: 75G
PROTEIN: 6G
CHOLESTEROL: 9MG
SODIUM: 151MG

FROZEN PEACH-GINGER YOGURT

SERVES: 4
WORKING TIME: 10 MINUTES
TOTAL TIME: 20 MINUTES PLUS FREEZING TIMES

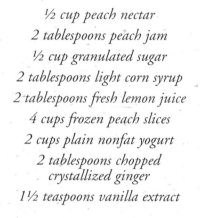

Peach
nectar and peach jam,
along with the sliced
fruit, make this a
triple-peach dessert.
Crystallized ginger
adds a lively "bite."

½ cup peach nectar
2 tablespoons peach jam
½ cup granulated sugar
2 tablespoons light corn syrup
2 tablespoons fresh lemon juice
4 cups frozen peach slices
2 cups plain nonfat yogurt
2 tablespoons chopped
crystallized ginger
1½ teaspoons vanilla extract

1. In a medium saucepan, combine the peach nectar, peach jam, sugar, corn syrup, and lemon juice and bring to a boil over medium heat. Reduce the heat to a simmer, add the peaches, cover, and cook until the fruit is very tender, about 8 minutes. Cool to room temperature.

2. Stir in the yogurt, ginger, and vanilla. Transfer to the canister of an ice cream maker and freeze according to the manufacturer's directions. Divide among 4 bowls and serve.

Helpful hint: You can make this frozen yogurt with fresh peaches instead of frozen: Blanch the fruit briefly in boiling water, peel, pit, and slice. You'll need about 1½ pounds of peaches to yield 4 cups of sliced fruit.

FAT: 0.4G/1%
CALORIES: 338
SATURATED FAT: 0.2G
CARBOHYDRATE: 79G
PROTEIN: 8G
CHOLESTEROL: 2MG
SODIUM: 110MG

CRUMBLES, CRÊPES, ETC.

5

NECTARINE-PEACH CRUMBLE

SERVES: 8
WORKING TIME: 20 MINUTES
TOTAL TIME: 55 MINUTES

A nectarine is not simply a fuzzless peach: Although the two fruits are closely related, nectarines are generally sweeter. We've used both in this luscious warm dessert (you could use all of one or the other), seasoning them with allspice and black pepper and spiking them with a shot of bourbon. A dollop of vanilla yogurt or ice milk would be delicious with the crumble.

1 pound nectarines, cut into ½-inch thick wedges

1⅓ cups firmly packed light brown sugar

¼ cup cornstarch

1 pound peaches, cut into ½-inch thick wedges

3 tablespoons bourbon, Scotch, or brandy

1 teaspoon grated lemon zest

2 tablespoons fresh lemon juice

⅛ teaspoon allspice

⅛ teaspoon freshly ground black pepper

⅓ cup old-fashioned rolled oats

⅓ cup flour

3 tablespoons unsalted butter, cut into small pieces

2 tablespoons reduced-fat sour cream

1. Preheat the oven to 375°. Spray a 6-cup glass or ceramic baking dish with nonstick cooking spray.

2. In a medium saucepan, combine half of the nectarines, 1 cup of the brown sugar, the cornstarch, and 1 tablespoon of water. Bring to a boil over medium heat. Remove from the heat and stir in the remaining nectarines, the peaches, bourbon, lemon zest, lemon juice, allspice, and pepper. Pour the mixture into the prepared baking dish.

3. In a medium bowl, stir together the oats, flour, and the remaining ⅓ cup brown sugar. With a pastry blender or 2 knives, cut in the butter and sour cream until the mixture resembles coarse crumbs. Spread the mixture over the fruit and bake for 30 minutes, or until browned and bubbly.

4. Serve warm or at room temperature.

Helpful hint: Old-fashioned rolled oats are whole, so they make a nice crisp crumble topping. You can substitute quick-cooking oats if necessary; however, because they are cut into pieces before rolling, they tend to get mushy. Instant oatmeal, which is cut even finer, should not be used.

FAT: 6G/20%
CALORIES: 275
SATURATED FAT: 3G
CARBOHYDRATE: 57G
PROTEIN: 2G
CHOLESTEROL: 13MG
SODIUM: 18MG

STRAWBERRY SHORTCAKE

SERVES: 8
WORKING TIME: 40 MINUTES
TOTAL TIME: 55 MINUTES PLUS DRAINING TIME

3 recipes Vanilla Yogurt Topping (p. 11, drained for 6 hours)

2 pints strawberries, quartered

¼ cup plus 2 tablespoons granulated sugar

1 cup all-purpose flour

1 cup cake flour

1 tablespoon baking powder

½ teaspoon baking soda

½ teaspoon salt

½ teaspoon ground ginger

4 tablespoons unsalted butter, cut into small pieces

¾ cup plus 1 tablespoon low-fat (1.5%) buttermilk

1 teaspoon confectioners' sugar

1. Make the vanilla yogurt cheese. Place the strawberries in a bowl, sprinkle with 2 tablespoons of the granulated sugar, and toss to combine. Preheat the oven to 425°. Spray an 8-inch round cake pan with nonstick cooking spray. In a large bowl, combine the all-purpose flour, cake flour, 2 tablespoons of the granulated sugar, the baking powder, baking soda, salt, and ginger. With a pastry blender or 2 knives, cut in the butter until the mixture resembles coarse crumbs. Make a well in the center and add the buttermilk. Stir with a fork until the dry ingredients are just moistened.

2. Turn the dough out onto a lightly floured surface and knead 6 or 8 times. Pat the dough evenly into the prepared cake pan and bake for 15 minutes, or until golden. Turn the shortcake out of the pan onto a wire rack to cool slightly.

3. Meanwhile, stir the remaining 2 tablespoons granulated sugar into the yogurt cheese. With a serrated knife, carefully split the shortcake horizontally. Place the whole bottom half of the shortcake on a serving plate. Place the top half on a work surface and cut into 8 wedges. Place half of the strawberries on top of the shortcake on the plate. Gently spread all but ¼ cup of the yogurt cheese over. Top with all but one of the remaining strawberries. Arrange the cake wedges on top of the filling and dust with the confectioners' sugar. Top with the remaining yogurt cheese and strawberry and serve.

FAT: 7G/24%
CALORIES: 259
SATURATED FAT: 4.1G
CARBOHYDRATE: 44G
PROTEIN: 6G
CHOLESTEROL: 19MG
SODIUM: 432MG

It takes courage to tamper with such a universal favorite as strawberry shortcake, but we're confident our lower-fat biscuits and tangy yogurt "cream" will draw raves. Those generous wedges of warm biscuit are made with low-fat buttermilk, which gives them a wonderfully tender texture; equal amounts of all-purpose flour and cake flour also contribute to their pleasing lightness.

A dessert of cooked fruit baked in a mold lined with slices of bread is called a "charlotte." Individual charlottes are highly appealing desserts—like little golden bandboxes with their buttery crust enclosing steaming, fragrant fruit. These pear and cranberry charlottes are served with a low-fat vanilla custard sauce.

Warm Pear Charlottes

WORKING TIME: 30 MINUTES

TOTAL TIME: 50 MINUTES

1 tablespoon plus 1 teaspoon
unsalted butter

2 tablespoons plus 2 teaspoons
granulated sugar

1½ pounds pears, peeled, cored,
and diced

½ cup dried cranberries, cherries,
or raisins

½ cup firmly packed light or
dark brown sugar

1 tablespoon fresh lemon juice

1 teaspoon grated lemon zest

20 slices (3½ x 3¼ inches) firm-
textured white sandwich bread

1½ teaspoons cornstarch mixed
with 1 tablespoon water

1 large egg

Vanilla Custard Sauce (p. 11)

1. Preheat the oven to 375°. Using ½ teaspoon of butter for each ramekin, butter eight 4-ounce ramekins or custard cups. Dust each ramekin with 1 teaspoon of the granulated sugar. In a large nonaluminum saucepan, combine the pears, cranberries, brown sugar, lemon juice, and lemon zest and bring to a boil over high heat. Reduce the heat to a simmer and cook, stirring occasionally, until the pears are softened, about 7 minutes.

2. Meanwhile, with a knife or a 2-inch round cookie cutter, cut out 2 circles from each of 8 slices of bread. Trim the crusts from the remaining 12 bread slices and cut each into 4 squares. Line the ramekins with bread: 1 bread circle on the bottom and 6 overlapping squares around the sides (see tip; top and middle photos).

3. Add the cornstarch mixture to the pear mixture and cook, whisking constantly, until slightly thickened, about 1 minute. In a medium bowl, lightly beat the egg. Whisk some hot pear mixture into the beaten egg. Whisk the warmed egg mixture back into the saucepan and cook over low heat, whisking, for 2 minutes.

4. Spoon the pear mixture into the bread-lined ramekins (see tip; bottom photo), top each with a bread circle, and place on a baking sheet. Bake for 25 minutes, or until the bread is golden. Meanwhile, make the custard sauce. Divide the custard sauce among 8 plates. Invert the charlottes, cut them in half, place on the sauce, and serve.

FAT: 6G/16%

CALORIES: 348

SATURATED FAT: 2.2G

CARBOHYDRATE: 69G

PROTEIN: 7G

CHOLESTEROL: 60MG

SODIUM: 292MG

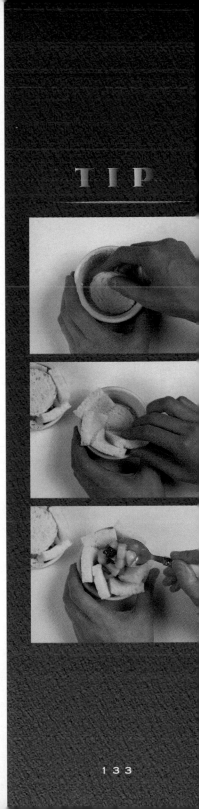

TIP

133

CRÊPES WITH GINGERED APPLE FILLING

SERVES: 6
WORKING TIME: 35 MINUTES
TOTAL TIME: 50 MINUTES PLUS CHILLING TIME

Maybe flaming crêpes Suzette are a bit too theatrical for a simple dinner at home, but warm crêpes filled with spicy poached apples are just the thing to complete a special meal. The apples are cooked in cider with just one tablespoon of butter. For an extra touch of color, set each scoop of frozen yogurt atop a few unpeeled apple slices.

⅔ cup flour
¾ cup low-fat (1%) milk
¼ cup plus 2 tablespoons granulated sugar
1 whole large egg
2 large egg whites
2 teaspoons vegetable oil
1 teaspoon vanilla extract
⅛ teaspoon salt
4 Granny Smith apples, peeled, cored, and cut into ½-inch-thick slices
1 teaspoon grated lemon zest
1 teaspoon cinnamon
½ teaspoon nutmeg
1 tablespoon unsalted butter
½ cup apple cider or apple juice
1 tablespoon minced crystallized ginger
2 cups vanilla nonfat frozen yogurt

1. In a food processor or blender, combine the flour, milk, 2 tablespoons of the sugar, the whole egg, egg whites, oil, vanilla, and salt and process until smooth. Scrape the batter into a bowl, cover, and refrigerate for 1 hour.

2. Preheat the oven to 200°. Spray an 8-inch nonstick skillet or crêpe pan with nonstick cooking spray and preheat over medium-high heat. Spoon 2 tablespoons of batter into the pan, tilting the pan to coat the bottom evenly with batter. Cook about 30 seconds, or until browned. Quickly turn the crêpe over and cook until browned on the second side, about 20 seconds. Transfer the crêpe to a heatproof plate and place in the oven. Repeat with the remaining batter, spraying the pan each time, to make 12 crêpes.

3. In a medium bowl, combine the apples, the remaining ¼ cup sugar, the lemon zest, cinnamon, and nutmeg, tossing to coat. In a large nonstick skillet, melt the butter over medium heat. Add the apples and cook until just softened, about 5 minutes. Add the cider and bring to a boil over high heat. Reduce the heat to a simmer, cover, and cook until the apples are tender, about 15 minutes. Remove from the heat and stir in the crystallized ginger.

4. Spoon about ¼ cup of hot apple filling into the center of each crêpe. Fold each crêpe into quarters and place 2 crêpes on each of 6 dessert plates. Spoon a scoop of frozen yogurt alongside and serve.

FAT: 7G/20%
CALORIES: 313
SATURATED FAT: 2G
CARBOHYDRATE: 58G
PROTEIN: 6G
CHOLESTEROL: 42MG
SODIUM: 77MG

CHOCOLATE SOUFFLÉ

SERVES: 6
WORKING TIME: 15 MINUTES
TOTAL TIME: 45 MINUTES

Your reputation as a cook will soar when you serve this handsome chocolate soufflé with its sophisticated raspberry sauce.

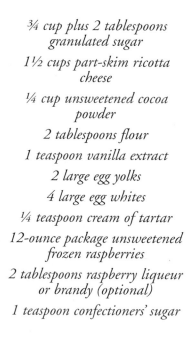

¾ cup plus 2 tablespoons granulated sugar

1½ cups part-skim ricotta cheese

¼ cup unsweetened cocoa powder

2 tablespoons flour

1 teaspoon vanilla extract

2 large egg yolks

4 large egg whites

¼ teaspoon cream of tartar

12-ounce package unsweetened frozen raspberries

2 tablespoons raspberry liqueur or brandy (optional)

1 teaspoon confectioners' sugar

1. Preheat the oven to 400°. Spray a 1½-quart soufflé dish with nonstick cooking spray. Dust the inside of the soufflé dish with 2 tablespoons of the granulated sugar; set aside.

2. In a food processor, combine ½ cup of the granulated sugar, the ricotta, cocoa powder, flour, vanilla, and egg yolks and process until smooth, about 1 minute. Transfer the ricotta mixture to a large bowl.

3. In a medium bowl, with an electric mixer, beat the egg whites until foamy. Add the cream of tartar and beat until stiff peaks form. Stir one-fourth of the egg whites into the ricotta mixture to lighten it, then gently fold in the remaining egg whites. Scrape into the prepared soufflé dish and bake for 30 minutes, or until puffed.

4. Meanwhile, in a food processor, combine the raspberries, the remaining ¼ cup sugar, and the liqueur and process to a smooth purée. Push the purée through a fine-mesh sieve to remove the seeds. Dust the soufflé with the confectioners' sugar and serve immediately with the raspberry sauce.

Helpful hint: An old cooking maxim says that guests should wait for the soufflé and not vice versa, and it holds true here: If a soufflé stands for more than a few minutes after it comes out of the oven, it may collapse.

FAT: 8G/24%
CALORIES: 296
SATURATED FAT: 3.8G
CARBOHYDRATE: 47G
PROTEIN: 12G
CHOLESTEROL: 90MG
SODIUM: 117MG

BLUEBERRY COBBLER

SERVES: 6
WORKING TIME: 30 MINUTES
TOTAL TIME: 1 HOUR 5 MINUTES

3 pints blueberries
2 cups plus 2 tablespoons flour
*½ cup plus 1 tablespoon
granulated sugar*
2 teaspoons grated lemon zest
2 tablespoons fresh lemon juice
1 tablespoon baking powder
½ teaspoon baking soda
1 teaspoon cinnamon
¼ teaspoon salt
*5 tablespoons unsalted butter,
cut into small pieces*
*¾ cup plus 2 tablespoons low-
fat (1.5%) buttermilk*

1. Preheat the oven to 400°. Place the blueberries in a 5-cup glass or ceramic baking dish. Sprinkle the blueberries with 2 table-spoons of the flour, all but 2 tablespoons of the sugar, the lemon zest, and lemon juice; toss to combine.

2. In a medium bowl, combine the remaining 2 cups flour, the remaining 2 tablespoons sugar, the baking powder, baking soda, cinnamon, and salt. With a pastry blender or 2 knives, cut in the butter until the mixture resembles coarse crumbs. Add the butter-milk all at once and stir until the dry ingredients are just moist-ened. Using a large spoon or a ¼-cup measure, drop the cobbler batter into 6 dumplings on top of the blueberry mixture.

3. Bake the cobbler for 30 to 35 minutes, or until the topping is lightly browned and the fruit mixture is bubbling. Serve warm or at room temperature.

Helpful hint: Light, quick handling is what produces tender, flaky biscuit dough: After adding the buttermilk, stir just long enough to moisten the dry ingredients (no more than about 30 seconds).

FAT: 11G/24%
CALORIES: 421
SATURATED FAT: 6.4G
CARBOHYDRATE: 76G
PROTEIN: 7G
CHOLESTEROL: 28MG
SODIUM: 468MG

Sometimes called "bird's-nest pudding," a cobbler is a pan of cooked fruit topped with golden biscuit "dumplings."

Coeur à la Crème

Serves: 4
Working time: 15 minutes
Total time: 15 minutes plus draining time

2 cups low-fat (1%) cottage cheese

8 ounces nonfat cream cheese

3 tablespoons reduced-fat cream cheese (Neufchâtel)

¼ cup reduced-fat sour cream

¾ cup granulated sugar

12-ounce package frozen unsweetened raspberries

1. In a food processor, combine the cottage cheese, nonfat cream cheese, and reduced-fat cream cheese and process until very smooth. Add the sour cream and ½ cup of the sugar, processing until well combined.

2. Line a heart-shaped coeur à la crème mold or a strainer with dampened cheesecloth, leaving a 2-inch overhang. Spoon the cheese mixture into the prepared mold, folding the overhang loosely on top to cover. Place on a plate to catch drips and refrigerate for at least 4 hours or overnight.

3. In a food processor, combine the raspberries and the remaining ¼ cup sugar and process to a smooth purée; push the purée through a fine-mesh sieve to remove the seeds.

4. To serve, unmold the coeur à la crème onto a serving plate and spoon the raspberry sauce around it.

Helpful hint: A coeur à la crème mold is a heart-shaped ceramic dish with holes in the bottom to allow whey to drain off. The mold is lined with cheesecloth, which leaves the surface of the coeur à la crème with a delicate linenlike texture.

Fat: 6g/14%
Calories: 375
Saturated Fat: 3g
Carbohydrate: 58g
Protein: 25g
Cholesterol: 21mg
Sodium: 793mg

To the French, a coeur à la crème (traditionally made with fresh cream cheese and heavy cream) is indisputably the perfect companion for the season's finest berries. We've paired our lightened version with a lush raspberry sauce, but you could serve the coeur with fresh raspberries or strawberries—or better still, with both sauce and fresh berries.

Humble cousins of the crêpe, blintzes are thin pancakes folded around a filling and then browned in butter. A lightly sweetened cottage-cheese filling is traditional; we've jazzed it up with chocolate and orange zest, a combination that may remind you of cannoli filling.

Cheese Blintzes

Serves: 4
Working time: 25 minutes
Total time: 1 hour 25 minutes

⅔ cup flour

2 tablespoons granulated sugar

½ teaspoon baking soda

¼ teaspoon salt

½ cup low-fat (1.5%) buttermilk

1 whole large egg

1 large egg white

2 teaspoons vegetable oil

1½ cups low-fat (1%) cottage cheese

¼ cup confectioners' sugar

1 ounce mini chocolate chips (about 2 tablespoons)

1 teaspoon grated orange zest

1 teaspoon vanilla extract

¼ cup plain nonfat yogurt

1 teaspoon unsalted butter

2 oranges, peeled and sectioned

1. In a blender or food processor, combine the flour, 1 tablespoon of the granulated sugar, the baking soda, salt, buttermilk, whole egg, egg white, oil, and ¼ cup of water and process until smooth. Pour the batter into a bowl, cover, and refrigerate for 1 hour.

2. Meanwhile, in a medium bowl, combine the cottage cheese, confectioners' sugar, chocolate chips, orange zest, and vanilla; set aside. In a small bowl, combine the yogurt and remaining 1 tablespoon granulated sugar; set aside.

3. Spray an 8-inch nonstick skillet or crêpe pan with nonstick cooking spray and preheat over medium-high heat. Spoon 2 tablespoons of batter into the pan, tilting the pan to coat the bottom evenly with batter. Cook for about 30 seconds, or until the blintz is browned on the bottom and the top is dry to the touch. Transfer the blintz to a plate. Repeat with the remaining batter, spraying the pan each time, to make 8 blintzes.

4. Spoon about 2 tablespoons of the cottage cheese mixture into the center of the browned side of each blintz. Roll up the blintzes (see tip). Spray a large nonstick skillet with nonstick cooking spray. Melt the butter over medium heat. Add the blintzes, seam-sides down, and cook until golden brown, turning once, about 3 minutes. Divide the blintzes among 4 plates and serve with the sweetened yogurt and the orange sections.

Fat: 10g/27%
Calories: 334
Saturated Fat: 3.3g
Carbohydrate: 44g
Protein: 18g
Cholesterol: 61mg
Sodium: 692mg

TIP

To fold the blintzes around the filling, first fold in two opposite sides to overlap the filling by about 1 inch; then fold in the two remaining sides to form a rectangular package.

POACHED PEARS WITH TWO SAUCES

SERVES: 4
WORKING TIME: 15 MINUTES
TOTAL TIME: 40 MINUTES

Today's chefs love to "paint" with dessert sauces—to drizzle and draw with bright purées and colorful creams. We've created a "partial eclipse" effect in black and white (chocolate sauce and vanilla ricotta sauce) as the setting for sherry-poached pears. You could also pool the light sauce (preferably on a dark plate) and drizzle the chocolate sauce over it in a pinwheel pattern.

½ cup dry sherry
½ cup granulated sugar
4 firm-ripe pears, peeled, halved, and cored
½ teaspoon vanilla extract
½ cup part-skim ricotta cheese
1½ ounces mini chocolate chips (about 3 tablespoons)

1. In a large skillet, combine the sherry, sugar, and 2 cups of water. Bring to a boil over medium heat, reduce to a simmer, and slip in the pears. Place a round of waxed paper directly on top of the pears (this will prevent discoloration) and simmer until tender, about 20 minutes. (Timing may vary depending upon the ripeness of the pears.)

2. With a slotted spatula, transfer the pears to a plate. Increase the heat to high and cook the poaching liquid until it is reduced to ½ cup, 5 to 10 minutes. Remove from the heat and stir in the vanilla. In a food processor, process the ricotta until smooth, about 1 minute. Add ¼ cup of the poaching liquid and process until combined. Cool to room temperature.

3. Add the chocolate chips and 1 tablespoon of water to the poaching liquid in the saucepan. Cook over low heat, stirring constantly, until the chocolate is just melted. Cool to room temperature.

4. Spoon a generous 1 tablespoon chocolate sauce on one side of each of 4 dessert plates. Fill in the other side of the plates with about 2 tablespoons of the ricotta sauce. Top with 2 pear halves and serve.

Helpful hints: A teaspoon is a good tool for coring halved pears. For a natural touch, leave the stems on the pears.

FAT: 6G/18%
CALORIES: 294
SATURATED FAT: 3.3G
CARBOHYDRATE: 60G
PROTEIN: 5G
CHOLESTEROL: 10MG
SODIUM: 42MG

Apple-Raisin Crumble

SERVES: 6
WORKING TIME: 20 MINUTES
TOTAL TIME: 1 HOUR 10 MINUTES

*O*ats and whole-wheat flour add a hearty note to this easy treat. Use tart apples such as Granny Smiths, Winesaps, or Gravensteins.

¼ cup plus 2 tablespoons all-purpose flour

2 tablespoons whole-wheat flour

2 tablespoons quick-cooking oats

3 tablespoons firmly packed light brown sugar

½ teaspoon cinnamon

⅛ teaspoon ground cloves

⅛ teaspoon salt

3 tablespoons cold unsalted butter, cut into small pieces

4 tart apples, peeled, cored, and coarsely chopped

¼ cup raisins (optional)

¼ cup granulated sugar

½ cup apple cider or juice

2 tablespoons fresh lemon juice

1. Preheat the oven to 375°. In a medium bowl, combine ¼ cup of the all-purpose flour, the whole-wheat flour, oats, brown sugar, cinnamon, cloves, and salt. With your fingers, rub in the butter until the mixture resembles coarse meal. Set the topping aside.

2. In an 8-cup glass or ceramic baking dish, combine the apples, raisins, granulated sugar, the remaining 2 tablespoons all-purpose flour, the apple cider, and lemon juice, tossing to thoroughly combine. Pat the filling into an even layer.

3. Sprinkle the topping over the apples and bake for 20 minutes. With a spatula, cut through the topping in several places to allow the juices to flow up and over the topping. Bake for 25 minutes, or until nicely browned and bubbling. Cool on a rack for 15 minutes before serving.

Helpful hint: You might like to accompany the crumble with a scoop of vanilla nonfat frozen yogurt or ice milk.

FAT: 6G/23%
CALORIES: 231
SATURATED FAT: 3.6G
CARBOHYDRATE: 64G
PROTEIN: 2G
CHOLESTEROL: 16MG
SODIUM: 96MG

FREEFORM APRICOT SOUFFLÉ

SERVES: 8
WORKING TIME: 20 MINUTES
TOTAL TIME: 35 MINUTES

¾ cup reduced-fat sour cream
½ cup low-fat (1%) cottage cheese
4 large egg yolks
2 tablespoons flour
1 cup apricot jam
¼ cup granulated sugar
2 tablespoons apricot brandy
1 teaspoon grated lemon zest
6 large egg whites, at room temperature

1. Preheat the oven to 425°. Spray a 10-inch nonstick skillet with an ovenproof handle with nonstick cooking spray.

2. In a food processor, combine the sour cream, cottage cheese, egg yolks, and flour and process until smooth, about 1 minute. Transfer the mixture to a large bowl and whisk in the jam, sugar, brandy, and lemon zest.

3. In a large bowl, with an electric mixer, beat the egg whites until stiff peaks form. Stir one-fourth of the egg whites into the cottage cheese mixture to lighten, then gently fold in the remaining whites. Scrape the mixture into the prepared skillet. Bake for about 15 minutes, or until golden brown and puffed.

Helpful hints: Egg whites separate more easily when they're cold, but they beat up to greater volume when they're at room temperature. Separate the eggs as soon as you take them out of the refrigerator, then set them aside in a covered bowl to come to room temperature before beating. (Refrigerate the yolks.) If the skillet you are using doesn't have an ovenproof handle, you can ovenproof it yourself by wrapping the handle in several layers of foil.

FAT: 6G/24%
CALORIES: 229
SATURATED FAT: 2.4G
CARBOHYDRATE: 37G
PROTEIN: 8G
CHOLESTEROL: 114MG
SODIUM: 130MG

This simplest of soufflés is made in a skillet for an unpretentious presentation. It bakes in just 15 minutes.

SOUR CHERRY CLAFOUTI

SERVES: 6
WORKING TIME: 10 MINUTES
TOTAL TIME: 50 MINUTES

A specialty of the Limousin region of central France, clafouti is a thick, oven-baked pancake studded with cherries or other fruits. It's a classic country dessert, made with pantry-staple ingredients and local produce. We've used sour cherries for their appealing tartness, and added ground toasted almonds to the batter.

1 cup jarred syrup-packed sour cherries, drained
1 teaspoon grated lemon zest
¼ cup slivered almonds, toasted
⅓ cup granulated sugar
1½ cups low-fat (1%) milk
⅔ cup flour
⅛ teaspoon salt
3 large eggs
1 teaspoon vanilla extract
1 teaspoon confectioners' sugar

1. Preheat the oven to 350°. Spray a 10-inch quiche dish (or other shallow 2-quart baking dish) with nonstick cooking spray. Place the cherries in the prepared dish. Stir in the lemon zest.

2. In a food processor, process the almonds and sugar until the almonds are finely ground. Add the milk, flour, salt, eggs, and vanilla and process until smooth. Pour the batter evenly over the cherries and bake for about 40 minutes, or until a knife inserted in the center comes out clean. Sprinkle with the confectioners' sugar and serve warm or at room temperature.

Helpful hint: You can substitute a cup of pitted fresh black cherries for the bottled cherries, if you like.

FAT: 6G/23%
CALORIES: 234
SATURATED FAT: 1.5G
CARBOHYDRATE: 37G
PROTEIN: 8G
CHOLESTEROL: 109MG
SODIUM: 112MG

What
fun it is to eat these
fruit dumplings! They
come to the table
looking quite
mysterious, but when
your fork pierces the
sugar-glazed crust a
puff of fragrant steam
hints at the
deliciousness within.
The plum halves are
filled with a mixture
of jam, brown sugar,
and butter that
permeates the fruit as
it bakes.

PLUM DUMPLINGS

SERVES: 4
WORKING TIME: 25 MINUTES
TOTAL TIME: 55 MINUTES

2 medium plums, halved and
pitted

1 tablespoon plus 1 teaspoon
unsalted butter

1 tablespoon firmly packed light
brown sugar

1 tablespoon plum jam

½ teaspoon vanilla extract

½ teaspoon grated lemon zest

1 cup flour

2 tablespoons granulated sugar

1 teaspoon baking powder

¼ teaspoon baking soda

¼ teaspoon salt

1 tablespoon reduced-fat sour
cream

⅓ cup low-fat (1.5%)
buttermilk

1 large egg white lightly beaten
with 1 teaspoon water

1. Preheat the oven to 400°. Place the plums, cut-sides up, on a work surface. In a small bowl, combine 1 teaspoon of the butter, the brown sugar, plum jam, vanilla, and lemon zest. Spoon the mixture into the hollows of the plums.

2. In a medium bowl, combine the flour, 4 teaspoons of the granulated sugar, the baking powder, baking soda, and salt. With a pastry blender or 2 knives, cut the remaining 1 tablespoon butter and the sour cream into the flour mixture until the mixture resembles coarse meal. Make a well in the center and stir in the buttermilk until just moistened. Transfer the dough to a lightly floured surface and roll out to an 8-inch square. Cut into four 4-inch squares.

3. Brush the dough squares with some of the egg white mixture. Place a plum half in the center of each piece of dough, pull the sides in, and seal to make a packet (see tip). Place on a baking sheet and brush with the remaining egg white mixture. Sprinkle the remaining 2 teaspoons granulated sugar on top and bake for about 30 minutes, or until golden brown. Divide the dumplings among 4 plates and serve.

Helpful hint: Use round clingstone plums rather than oval, freestone Italian plums (prune plums) for this recipe. Some possibilities are Friars, Simkas, Santa Rosas, Larodas, El Dorados, and Queen Anns.

FAT: 5G/18%
CALORIES: 245
SATURATED FAT: 2.9G
CARBOHYDRATE: 44G
PROTEIN: 6G
CHOLESTEROL: 13MG
SODIUM: 365MG

TIP

To enclose the plums in the dough, bring the four points of the dough square together on top of the fruit twisting the tip to seal. Pinch the dough together at each corner, but do not pinch the long edges together—this way the natural gaps between the edges can act as steam vents.

WINTER FRUIT COMPOTE

SERVES: 6
WORKING TIME: 20 MINUTES
TOTAL TIME: 35 MINUTES

½ cup granulated sugar

1-inch piece of fresh ginger, peeled and very thinly slivered

2 Granny Smith apples, peeled, cored, and cut into wedges

1 firm-ripe pear, peeled, cored, and cut into ¾-inch chunks

½ cup dried apricots

2 cups fresh or frozen cranberries

2 oranges, peeled and sectioned

1. In a large saucepan, combine the sugar, 1½ cups of water, and the ginger. Bring to a boil over high heat. Add the apples, pear, and apricots. Reduce the heat to low and simmer, uncovered, until the fruit is softened, about 5 minutes.

2. Add the cranberries and cook, stirring occasionally, until the cranberries pop, about 5 minutes. Stir in the orange sections and remove from the heat. Transfer the compote to a bowl and serve warm or at room temperature.

Helpful hint: You can use any flavorful apple in this recipe. Some less familiar ones to try are Empires, Ida Reds, Macouns, Jonathans, Cortlands, and Winesaps. If you don't find them at the supermarket, visit a farmers' market, orchard, or roadside fruit stand.

FAT: 1G/5%
CALORIES: 172
SATURATED FAT: 0G
CARBOHYDRATE: 44G
PROTEIN: 1G
CHOLESTEROL: 0MG
SODIUM: 2MG

Warm fruit compote, redolent of ginger, is a lovely cold weather dessert; you might offer vanilla yogurt or sour cream with the compote, and pass a plate of crisp, simple cookies. The colorful fruit mixture would also be perfect at a brunch, served with warm muffins or biscuits. Stock up on cranberries at holiday time, when they're widely available, and keep them in the freezer.

Orange Ricotta Soufflé

Serves: 4
Working time: 15 minutes
Total time: 45 minutes

Since egg whites are the hard-working ingredient in a soufflé—they make it rise and puff—we've dispensed with most of the yolks in this recipe (and thus most of the fat from the yolks). Low-fat cottage cheese and part-skim ricotta give the soufflé body and creamy flavor, the perfect foil for the double citrus impact of orange zest and orange liqueur.

2 cups low-fat (1%) cottage cheese

1 cup part-skim ricotta cheese

½ cup plus 2 tablespoons granulated sugar

¼ cup flour

2 tablespoons orange liqueur (such as Grand Marnier) or orange juice

1 teaspoon grated orange zest

1 large egg yolk

3 large egg whites

¼ teaspoon salt

1. Preheat the oven to 375°. Spray a 1½-quart soufflé dish with non-stick cooking spray; set aside. In a food processor, process the cottage cheese and ricotta until very smooth, about 2 minutes. Add ½ cup of the granulated sugar, the flour, orange liqueur, orange zest, and egg yolk and process until well combined, about 30 seconds. Transfer to a bowl.

2. In a medium bowl, with an electric mixer, beat the egg whites with the salt until foamy. Beat in the remaining 2 tablespoons granulated sugar, 1 tablespoon at a time, until the whites are stiff and shiny, about 8 minutes. Gently fold the egg whites into the ricotta mixture and spoon into the prepared mold, smoothing the top. Bake for 30 minutes, or until puffed and golden brown.

Helpful hint: For best results, begin beating the egg whites with the mixer on low speed, then increase the speed to high after adding the sugar.

Fat: 8g/20%
Calories: 366
Saturated Fat: 4.2g
Carbohydrate: 46g
Protein: 25g
Cholesterol: 77mg
Sodium: 714mg

GLOSSARY

Almond extract—A concentrated flavoring made from the oil of bitter almonds. This potent extract lets you make almond-flavored desserts without using a lot of the nuts themselves, which are high in fat. It's worth the extra cost to buy pure (natural) almond extract; imitation almond flavorings may be harsh and unpleasant.

Applesauce, sweetened and unsweetened—A cooked purée of fresh apples, with or without added sugar. Applesauce plays an important role in healthy baking in that it can actually be substituted for fat in simple cakes, cookies, muffins, and quick breads. The soluble fiber in apples, along with other substances in the fruit, can mimic the qualities usually supplied by shortening in baked goods.

Apricot, dried—A dried fruit with intensely concentrated apricot flavor. Some dried apricots are treated with sulfur dioxide to preserve their color; the unsulfured variety is darker in color and richer in flavor. To plump dried apricots, soak them in warm water, orange juice, or brandy.

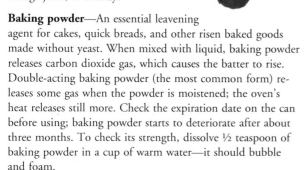

Baking powder—An essential leavening agent for cakes, quick breads, and other risen baked goods made without yeast. When mixed with liquid, baking powder releases carbon dioxide gas, which causes the batter to rise. Double-acting baking powder (the most common form) releases some gas when the powder is moistened; the oven's heat releases still more. Check the expiration date on the can before using; baking powder starts to deteriorate after about three months. To check its strength, dissolve ½ teaspoon of baking powder in a cup of warm water—it should bubble and foam.

Baking soda—A leavening agent (bicarbonate of soda) that reacts with acid ingredients such as buttermilk, yogurt, or molasses. Baking soda not only leavens baked goods, it also neutralizes acidity, resulting in milder, sweeter, flavors. Baking soda immediately begins to produce carbon dioxide gas when it is mixed with liquid, so batters and doughs made with it should be baked right after they're mixed.

Butter, unsalted—A solid fat made by churning heavy cream. Although it is high in fat (about 12 grams per tablespoon), butter's inimitable flavor makes it a must for certain baking recipes (recipes in this book may call for a combination of butter and a less saturated fat, or butter and a fat substitute such as low-fat cream cheese or applesauce). Unsalted butter is preferred for baking because of its fresher, cleaner taste. If you buy butter that you don't plan to use right away, wrap the package in foil, or place it in a plastic bag, and freeze it for up to six months.

Buttermilk—A tart, tangy milk product made by adding a special bacterial culture to nonfat or low-fat milk. Buttermilk's acidity inhibits the development of gluten (a tough protein in flour), so baked goods made with it turn out tender. Our recipes call for 1.5% buttermilk. In a pinch, make your own "buttermilk" by combining 1 tablespoon lemon juice or vinegar with enough 1% milk to measure 1 cup.

Chocolate chips—Small morsels of chocolate, usually semisweet. Chocolate chips, which come in regular, mini, and large sizes, are used to dot cookies and cakes and also are a convenient form for melting, since they don't need to be chopped. You'll find directions for melting chocolate chips on the stovetop and in the microwave on page 9.

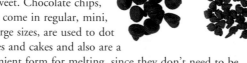

Chocolate, German sweet—A dark, sweet chocolate for cooking and baking. German sweet chocolate is sold in 4-ounce bars in the baking-ingredients aisle of the supermarket. You can use another brand of dark, sweet chocolate, but don't substitute milk, bittersweet, or unsweetened chocolate.

Cocoa powder, unsweetened—The dried, powdered form of pure chocolate from which most of the fat has been removed. Cocoa is a boon to healthy dessert-making since it is low in fat when compared with solid chocolate. "Dutch-process" cocoa is treated with alkali, which neutralizes some of the acid in the cocoa, resulting in a less harsh flavor; it is usually darker in color than regular cocoa powder.

Corn syrup—A thick, clear, intensely sweet syrup made from cornstarch. Corn syrup comes in light and dark forms; the light version has a more neutral flavor. Corn syrup helps prevent crystallization in frozen desserts. It also helps keep baked goods moist, and can replace part of the fat in some recipes.

Cornstarch—A fine flour made from the endosperm of the corn kernel. Cornstarch is an effective thickener and is used in puddings, custards, pie fillings, and frozen desserts for creamy thickness without added fat.

Cottage cheese—A tangy, spoonable fresh cheese, available in creamed (highest in fat), low-fat, and nonfat forms. Puréed low-fat cottage cheese can stand in for cream cheese or ricotta in cheesecakes, creamy pie fillings, and puddings to keep them nutritionally sensible.

Cream of tartar—A white, powdery natural fruit acid that is a by-product of winemaking. Cream of tartar is invaluable for increasing the volume and stability of beaten egg whites. Also, when combined with baking soda, it releases carbon dioxide to lighten batters.

Cream cheese, Neufchâtel and nonfat—Lower-fat forms of a spreadable, mild-flavored white cheese. Neufchâtel has one-third less fat than regular cream cheese. These cheeses can be judiciously substituted for regular cream cheese in cheesecakes, frostings, pastry, and frozen desserts.

Eggs—A basic ingredient in cakes, cookies, pie fillings, and custards. Egg whites, which are fat-free, whip up into an airy foam that supplies the structure for angel food cakes and meringues. Egg yolks can sometimes be omitted from cake and cookie batters, but most recipes will turn out better if you include at least one egg yolk. Always store eggs in the refrigerator, preferably in their original carton.

Evaporated milk, regular and skimmed—Canned, unsweetened, homogenized milk, whole or with 100 percent of the fat removed. Used in baking or cooking, it adds the richness of cream with much less fat. Store cans at room temperature for up to 6 months until opened, then transfer to a covered container and refrigerate for up to 1 week.

Flour, all-purpose—A basic baking ingredient made by milling and sifting the inner part of the wheat kernel; a combination of hard and soft wheat is used, making this flour suitable for most recipes. Some all-purpose flour is chemically bleached: It looks whiter (unbleached flour is a creamy beige color), but your choice of bleached or unbleached flour will have no effect on the finished product.

Flour, cake—A type of flour that is milled from soft wheat, and is thus lower in gluten. Cake flour is used in baking delicate cakes since it gives them a fine, tender crumb. If you need to substitute all-purpose flour, place 2 tablespoons cornstarch in a 1-cup dry measure and spoon in enough all-purpose flour to equal 1 level cup.

Flour, whole wheat—A type of flour milled from wheat kernels with their bran layer and germ intact. It is higher in fiber than white flour. Whole-wheat flour makes baked goods more healthful, but because it is heavier and darker than regular flour, it should not be substituted for all the white flour in a recipe. It is, however, usually safe to replace about one-third of the all-purpose flour in a recipe with whole-wheat flour. (Never substitute whole-wheat flour for cake flour.) Because whole grains can become rancid, whole-wheat flour should be stored in the refrigerator or freezer, where it will keep for six to eight months.

Gelatin, unflavored—A powder made from animal protein, used to thicken and set various desserts. For best results, dissolve the gelatin in cold water before adding it to a hot liquid. Certain fresh fruits, such as pineapple, kiwi, and papaya, contain an enzyme that prevents gelatin from gelling. Gelatin comes in 1¼-ounce envelopes; be sure to measure carefully the amount called for in the recipe: Too little, and the mixture won't set; too much, and it will be too stiff.

Ginger, crystallized—A confection made from fresh ginger that has been chopped into coarse pieces, cooked in syrup, and then coated with sugar. Sweet-hot in flavor, it is a lively addition to desserts. Look for it in jars in the spice section of the supermarket and in bulk at candy stores, gourmet shops, and Asian groceries (it's usually much cheaper when purchased in bulk).

Ginger, dried ground—A "warm" spice made by drying and pulverizing gingerroot, which is grown mainly in Jamaica. A standard ingredient in spicy desserts, ginger is used in fruit compotes and crisps, spice cookies and cakes, pumpkin pie, and, of course, gingersnaps. Like all spices, ginger loses its flavor with time; buy a new jar if the ginger in your spice rack lacks a lively bite.

Juice, fruit—The liquid extracted from apples, oranges, lemons, and the like, used as flavorings in desserts. Fruit juices also supply the acid component needed in some baking recipes. Whereas sugar contributes only sweetness, the juices of sweet fruits, such as apples, grapes, and pineapples, can simultaneously sweeten and underscore the fruit flavor of a dessert. Tart citrus juices—orange, lemon, lime, tangerine, and grapefruit—often serve as a counterpoint to sweetness. While citrus juices pack the most flavor when freshly squeezed, other fruit juices come in convenient canned, bottled, and frozen forms.

Mango—A yellow-skinned fruit with vivid orange flesh and an unmistakable sweet-tart flavor. Although they originated in India, mangoes are now cultivated in other parts of the world. Mangoes can range from about 10 ounces to about four pounds in weight; all have a large, flat seed from which the flesh must be cut away. An unripe mango can be placed in a brown paper bag at room temperature to ripen. When ripe, the fruit will give to slight pressure and will have a rich, flowery fragrance.

Nectarine—A close cousin of the peach, with smooth, crimson-blushed, golden skin and yellow flesh. Nectarines may be either clingstone or freestone: The freestone varieties are easier to pit and slice. Choose nectarines with good, deep golden color under the red blush: Avoid greenish fruits. Soften hard nectarines by keeping them in a paper bag for a few days at room temperature. Nectarines may be substituted for peaches in most recipes.

Peach—A sweet summer tree fruit with a large central stone and fuzzy skin. Peaches may be freestone, semi-freestone, or clingstone, but almost all peaches sold fresh in supermarkets are freestone—the fruit can be halved and pitted very easily (clingstones, which have firmer flesh, are processed for canning). It's best to buy local peaches in season—they're picked closer to full ripeness so they'll be sweeter. When buying peaches that have been shipped from a distance, choose those that are not rock-hard and have a warm cream-to-yellow color with a rosy tinge. Keep them at room temperature until they yield to finger pressure and are sweetly fragrant.

Raspberries, fresh and frozen—Perfumy, thimble-sized red, black, or golden berries with hollow cores. Fresh raspberries are particularly perishable, so they're quite expensive out of season. Locally grown berries will be tastier as well as cheaper than those shipped by distant growers. Fortunately, unsweetened frozen red raspberries are widely available in supermarkets and can be substituted for fresh in many recipes. When buying fresh berries, check in the bottom of the basket, where spoiled fruits may be hidden. Store raspberries in the refrigerator, covered, for no longer than 1 to 2 days.

Ricotta cheese—A fresh, creamy white, Italian cheese with a grainier texture than cottage cheese and a slightly sweet flavor. Available in whole-milk and part-skim versions, it can enrich a variety of desserts, standing in for mascarpone (a super-rich Italian cream cheese), or, when puréed, for the heavy cream in a sauce or frozen dessert.

Sour cream—A tart, thick dairy product, made by treating sweet cream with a lactic acid culture. Regular sour cream contains at least 18 percent milk fat by volume; reduced-fat sour cream contains 4 percent fat; nonfat sour cream is, of course, fat-free. Sour cream is a wonderfully rich-tasting, tangy dessert ingredient; it also makes a tasty topping, offering a tart counterpoint to sweetness. The reduced-fat version can be substituted for regular sour cream in most recipes; use nonfat sour cream cautiously, since it behaves differently, especially in baking.

Sugar, brown—Granulated white sugar mixed with molasses for a softer texture and fuller flavor than plain white sugar. Dark brown sugar, made with more molasses, has a richer, sweeter flavor, although the two can be used interchangeably in most recipes. To keep brown sugar soft, store it in an airtight container with a slice of bread.

Sugar, confectioners'—Also called powdered sugar, this is granulated white sugar that has been crushed to a powder; a little cornstarch is usually mixed in to prevent caking. The most common form is 10X (ultrafine); 4X can be used instead. Confectioners' sugar is frequently used in frostings, glazes, candies, and beverages because it dissolves readily and blends smoothly. It also makes a delicate finishing touch for unfrosted cakes and cookies. Recipes often direct you to sift confectioners' sugar because it tends to be lumpy.

Sugar, granulated—White sugar, made from either sugar beets or sugarcane, that has been processed to form fine, crystalline particles. Used in many desserts, granulated sugar not only sweetens foods but also makes baked goods more tender and helps them brown.

Sugar, superfine—A finer form of granulated sugar. Superfine sugar, also called bar sugar, is used in recipes where the sugar must dissolve more quickly. If you can't find it where you shop, substitute granulated sugar or process it in the food processor to approximate the texture of superfine.

Tapioca, quick-cooking—The granular form of a starchy flour derived from the root of the cassava plant; this form of tapioca doesn't require presoaking. Tapioca, which thickens when combined with a hot liquid, serves as the base for low-fat puddings and can also be used to thicken juices in fruit pies.

Vanilla—The dried pod of a climbing orchid. A vanilla bean can be simmered in liquids such as milk for custards, or the pod can be split and the seeds scraped into cake batter. To reuse the bean after cooking, rinse, blot dry, and store in a sugar canister, where it will also impart a vanilla flavor to the sugar. Pure vanilla extract is a convenient substitute, but imitation vanilla extract has an unpleasant aftertaste.

Yogurt, vanilla low-fat—A sweetened, flavored cultured milk product that contains 2 to 4 grams of fat per cup. Tasty just as it comes from the carton, vanilla yogurt is a useful dessert ingredient, too. When drained (see page 11), it thickens, and can be used as a dessert topping or cake filling.

Zest, citrus—The very thin, outermost colored part of the rind of citrus fruits; it contains strongly flavored oils. Zest gives an intense true fruit taste to desserts—more flavor than juices can impart. Remove the zest with a grater, citrus zester, or vegetable peeler; be careful to scrape off only the colored layer and not the bitter white pith beneath it.

INDEX

Time-Life Books is a division of Time Life Inc.

TIME LIFE INC.

PRESIDENT and CEO: George Artandi

TIME-LIFE BOOKS

PRESIDENT: John D. Hall
PUBLISHER/MANAGING EDITOR: Neil Kagan

GREAT TASTE–LOW FAT
Desserts

DEPUTY EDITOR: Marion Ferguson Briggs
DIRECTOR, NEW PRODUCT DEVELOPMENT: Quentin S. McAndrew
MARKETING DIRECTOR: Robin B. Shuster

Consulting Editor: Catherine Boland Hackett

Vice President, Director of Finance: Christopher Hearing
Vice President, Book Production: Marjann Caldwell
Director of Operations: Eileen Bradley
Director of Photography and Research: John Conrad Weiser
Director of Editorial Administration: Judith W. Shanks
Production Manager: Marlene Zack
Quality Assurance Manager: James King
Library: Louise D. Forstall

Design for Great Taste–Low Fat by David Fridberg of
Miles Fridberg Molinaroli, Inc.

 REBUS, INC.

PUBLISHER: Rodney M. Friedman
EDITORIAL DIRECTOR: Charles L. Mee

Editorial Staff for *Desserts*
Director, Recipe Development and Photography: Grace Young
Editorial Director: Kate Slate
Senior Recipe Developer: Sandra Rose Gluck
Recipe Developer: Marianne Zanzarella
Writer: Bonnie J. Slotnick
Managing Editor: Julee Binder Shapiro
Editorial Assistant: James W. Brown, Jr.
Nutritionists: Hill Nutrition Associates

Art Director: Timothy Jeffs
Photographer: Lisa Koenig
Photographer's Assistants: Alix Berenberg, Katie Bleacher Everard,
    Rainer Fehringer, Petra Liebetanz, Wayne Parry
Food Stylists: Karen Pickus, Karen Tack
Assistant Food Stylists: Mako Antonishek, Charles Davis, Ellie Ritt
Prop Stylist: Debrah Donahue
Prop Coordinator: Karin Martin

Library of Congress Cataloging-in-Publication Data

Desserts.
    p.   cm. -- (Great taste, low fat)
Includes index.
ISBN 0-7835-4560-6
1. Desserts. 2. Low-fat diet--Recipes. 3. Quick and easy cookery.
I. Time-Life Books. II. Series.
TX773.D47743   1996
641.8'6--dc20   96-17871
                                                          CIP

OTHER PUBLICATIONS

COOKING
WEIGHT WATCHERS® SMART CHOICE RECIPE COLLECTION
WILLIAMS-SONOMA KITCHEN LIBRARY

DO IT YOURSELF
THE TIME-LIFE COMPLETE GARDENER
HOME REPAIR AND IMPROVEMENT
THE ART OF WOODWORKING
FIX IT YOURSELF

TIME-LIFE KIDS
FAMILY TIME BIBLE STORIES
LIBRARY OF FIRST QUESTIONS AND ANSWERS
A CHILD'S FIRST LIBRARY OF LEARNING
I LOVE MATH
NATURE COMPANY DISCOVERIES
UNDERSTANDING SCIENCE & NATURE

HISTORY
THE AMERICAN STORY
VOICES OF THE CIVIL WAR
THE AMERICAN INDIANS
LOST CIVILIZATIONS
MYSTERIES OF THE UNKNOWN
TIME FRAME
THE CIVIL WAR
CULTURAL ATLAS

SCIENCE/NATURE
VOYAGE THROUGH THE UNIVERSE

*For information on and a full description of any of the Time-Life Books series
listed above, please call 1-800-621-7026 or write:*
Reader Information
Time-Life Customer Service
P.O. Box C-32068
Richmond, Virginia 23261-2068

METRIC CONVERSION CHARTS

VOLUME EQUIVALENTS
(fluid ounces/milliliters and liters)

US	Metric
1 tsp	5 ml
1 tbsp (½ fl oz)	15 ml
¼ cup (2 fl oz)	60 ml
⅓ cup	80 ml
½ cup (4 fl oz)	120 ml
⅔ cup	160 ml
¾ cup (6 fl oz)	180 ml
1 cup (8 fl oz)	240 ml
1 qt (32 fl oz)	950 ml
1 qt + 3 tbsps	1 L
1 gal (128 fl oz)	4 L

Conversion formula
Fluid ounces X 30 = milliliters
1000 milliliters = 1 liter

WEIGHT EQUIVALENTS
(ounces and pounds/grams and kilograms)

US	Metric
¼ oz	7 g
½ oz	15 g
¾ oz	20 g
1 oz	30 g
8 oz (½ lb)	225 g
12 oz (¾ lb)	340 g
16 oz (1 lb)	455 g
35 oz (2.2 lbs)	1 kg

Conversion formula
Ounces X 28.35 = grams
1000 grams = 1 kilogram

LINEAR EQUIVALENTS
(inches and feet/centimeters and meters)

US	Metric
¼ in	.75 cm
½ in	1.5 cm
¾ in	2 cm
1 in	2.5 cm
6 in	15 cm
12 in (1 ft)	30 cm
39 in	1 m

Conversion formula
Inches X 2.54 = centimeters
100 centimeters = 1 meter

TEMPERATURE EQUIVALENTS
(Fahrenheit/Celsius)

US	Metric
0° (freezer temperature)	-18°
32° (water freezes)	0°
98.6°	37°
180° (water simmers*)	82°
212° (water boils*)	100°
250° (low oven)	120°
350° (moderate oven)	175°
425° (hot oven)	220°
500° (very hot oven)	260°

*at sea level

Conversion formula
Degrees Fahrenheit minus
32 ÷ 1.8 = degrees Celsius